# The Glen '98

50 Years

*of*

Road Racing Excellence

# TABLE *of* CONTENTS

## "Gentlemen, to your cars!"

The Queen Catharine Cup race during the 1951 Grand Prix used a LeMans-style start. This was the third and final year the Glen used a "running" start for one of its support races, using the method popularized by the 24 hours of LeMans. Note the LeSabre, a General Motors concept car, parked near the sidewalk.

•••


Foreword by Cameron Argetsinger ..... 3
Important Dates in Watkins Glen History ..... 4
A Welcome from John Saunders ..... 5
Kendall ..... 6
Zippo ..... 7
Introduction by Jackie Stewart ..... 8

Chapter One — *Racing in the Streets* ..... 11
Chapter Two — *Years of Transition* ..... 37
Chapter Three — *The Formula One Years* ..... 63
Chapter Four — *Professional Sports Car Racing* ..... 129
Chapter Five — *The Glen is Back* ..... 165
Chapter Six — *NASCAR Comes North* ..... 187

# ACKNOWLEDGEMENTS

UMI Publications, Inc. in conjunction with Watkins Glen International is proud to bring you The Glen '98 — 50 Years of Road Racing Excellence, the official publication commissioned by Watkins Glen International to celebrate 50 years of road racing at the famed circuit. The best photography available has been assembled to make this half-century tribute a book you will want to refer to again and again.

Our special thanks go to the team at Watkins Glen, including Roger Curtis, J.J. O'Malley, John Saunders and photographers Ade Ketchum, Hal Crocker, Dave Friedman and Bill Green. Without their knowledge, guidance and enthusiasm, this book would have never happened.

We also would like to extend our gratitude to all the photographers involved in providing amazing documentation of America's most celebrated road-course. Special Thanks to: *Al Horowitz, Al Tarlach, Alix LaFontant, Arthur H. Richards Jr. Collection, Ben Hendee, C.M. Durland, Bill Cox, Cameron Argetsinger Collection, Cathy Keister, Charles A. Lytle Jr., Charles Berch, Charles Spear, Darryl Moran, Dave Hohenshilt, David Chobat, Dick Robinson, Don O'Reilly, Don Romeo, Elmer Forsythe, Fred Proper Sr., High Sierra Photos, J&H Photos, J.J. O'Malley, Jim Walsh, John Hood, Joe Jennings, John Doddato, John Domaleski, John Hammond, John Hood, Lyn Rexford, Mike O'Malley, Nate Mecha, Oscar Koveleski, Rob Tarlach, Rodney Curtis, Roger Capone, Roger Curtis, Roger T. Patterson, Steve Pike, Stuart P. Luther, T.J. Tristan, Tom Bauman, Tom Cooley, Tom Erwin, Tom James, Tony Mezzacca, Sue Morton, Watkins Glen Racing Archives, Wayne Keister, William Green Collection.*

***Staff: Publisher/President:*** *Ivan Mothershead;* ***Associate Publisher/Executive Vice President:*** *Charlie Keiger;* ***Vice President:*** *Rick Peters;* ***Controller:*** *Lewis Patton ;* ***Advertising Manager:*** *Mark Cantey;* ***Advertising Executive:*** *Paul Kaperonis;* ***Managing Editor:*** *Ward Woodbury;* ***Copy & Photo Editing:*** *Roger Curtis, J.J. O'Malley, Ann Connor, Mike Argetsinger;* ***Art Direction:*** *Brett Shippy;* ***Senior Designers:*** *Mike McBride and Paul Bond;* ***Manager of Information Systems:*** *Henry Boardman;* ***Customer Service Representatives:*** *Mary Cartee, Carla Greene.*

ISBN 0-943860-14-8

# FOREWORD

by CAMERON ARGETSINGER

I remember exactly where I was at one o'clock, Saturday, October 2, 1948. I was seated in my red TC MG on the grid in front of the Schuyler County Court House, ready for the drop of the green flag to signal the start of the first race to be held in Watkins Glen, which was also the first post-World War II road race in the United States. I knew I would never forget the excitement of the moment, the culmination of a year's planning.

What is remarkable is that 50 years later so many other people remember the excitement of that day. What is satisfactory is to know there has been racing at The Glen every year since 1948. Bringing Formula Libre to The Glen in 1958, as an introduction to the Formula One United States Grand Prix in 1961, which was the realization of a dream that inspired me to organize the first race.

There were many people who made it possible to organize and continue through the years. To name the obvious ones is a pleasure: Don Brubaker, Lester and Flossie Smalley, Art Richards, Mayor Alan D. Erway, Bill Milliken, Henry Valent, Nick Fraboni, Malcolm Currie, James Riesbeck, Bill Ellison and John Saunders. Then there are the thousands of others in the community and in the sport who worked to make racing at The Glen the glorious success it has enjoyed for 50 years.

The triumphs of The Glen with sports cars, Formula One and now NASCAR are preserved by Bill Green and J.J. O'Malley in this meticulously researched history of The Glen. The book will serve as a reference for years to come for the scholars of the sport. For me, it is an interesting story filled with nostalgia and adventure. We who love the sport and The Glen owe a debt of gratitude to Bill and J.J. for keeping the record straight.

> "What is satisfactory is to know there has been racing at the Glen every year since 1948."
>
> CAMERON ARGETSINGER

# Important Dates

## in Watkins Glen History

| | |
|---|---|
| *Oct. 2, 1948* | First Watkins Glen Grand Prix on 6.6-mile circuit on public roads. |
| *Sept. 19, 1956* | First permanent circuit opens. |
| *August 4, 1957* | Buck Baker wins first professional race at The Glen, a NASCAR Grand National event. |
| *Oct. 8, 1961* | Innes Ireland wins The Glen's first Formula One event. |
| *Sept. 3, 1965* | Graham Hill wins third straight U.S. Grand Prix. |
| *Oct. 3, 1971* | Francois Cevert wins U.S. Grand Prix, first race on rebuilt 3.377-mile circuit. |
| *Oct. 5, 1980* | Alan Jones wins final U.S. Grand Prix at The Glen. |
| *Oct. 4, 1981* | Rick Mears wins CART Indy car race, final event under Watkins Glen Grand Prix Corporation ownership. |
| *Sept. 20, 1983* | Watkins Glen International announced as new owner of race track, a joint venture between Corning Enterprises and the International Speedway Corporation. |
| *July 7, 1984* | Al Holbert, Derek Bell and Jim Adams win IMSA Camel Continental, first race at The Glen under WGI ownership. |
| *July 6, 1984* | Al Holbert and Derek Bell win third consecutive Camel Continental; Geoff Bodine wins in GTO class. |
| *August 10, 1986* | Tim Richmond wins first Budweiser at The Glen NASCAR Winston Cup race. |
| *June 29, 1990* | Terry Labonte wins WGI's first NASCAR Busch Series race. |
| *June 27, 1992* | Davy Jones qualifies for the Camel Continental at 150.334 mph in Jaguar XJR-14, fastest lap in North American road racing history. |
| *August 13, 1995* | Mark Martin wins third consecutive Bud at The Glen. |
| *August 9-11, 1996* | Dale Earnhardt breaks track NASCAR Winston Cup qualifying record two weeks after Talladega injuries, finishes sixth in Bud at The Glen won by local native Geoff Bodine. |
| *August 25, 1996* | Ron Hornaday wins Parts America 150, first NASCAR Craftsman Truck Series race at The Glen. |
| *March 4, 1997* | International Speedway Corporation announces full ownership of Watkins Glen International. |
| *August 10, 1997* | Jeff Gordon wins Bud at The Glen, first career road course victory. |

# WELCOME

*from* JOHN SAUNDERS

> This compilation illustrates the history of the men and machines that made Watkins Glen a world famous center of road racing ...
>
> JOHN SAUNDERS

Welcome to Watkins Glen!

On behalf of the team at Watkins Glen International, I invite you to celebrate fifty years of motor racing in Watkins Glen, New York.

Watkins Glen, with all of its charms and scenic beauty, was host to the first road race in the United States following World War II. The 1948 Watkins Glen Grand Prix was just the beginning of great things to come, a beginning championed by the collective vision of Cameron Argetsinger, Don Brubaker, Lester Smalley, and so many other dedicated, hard-working residents of Schuyler County, New York. Since the day in 1948, "the day they stopped the trains," Watkins Glen has emerged as one of the premier road racing communities in the world.

This compilation illustrates the history of the men and machines that made Watkins Glen a world famous center of road racing, and highlights the past fifty years from World Champions to NASCAR champions, from formula cars to stock cars.

This book is a fitting tribute to the heroes, their teams and families, as well as the unified dedication and commitment of a very, very special community, the residents of Schuyler County. It was the efforts of these people that made the fifty years of racing at Watkins Glen possible.

# A Word *from* Kendall

## Gregory Booth

Dear Friends and Associates of Watkins Glen International,

I am delighted that Kendall has been fortunate enough to have been involved with The Glen for nearly fifty years. I am even more delighted that we were at Kendall now that we have an opportunity to celebrate with The Glen and it's fans on the 50th Anniversary of this wonderful racing facility.

My relationship with The Glen dates back to the mid-sixties when I attended my first Can-Am race. I was thrilled by not only the racing, but with the entire Watkins Glen experience. The excitement of just being at the track and experiencing all that goes on around the track was without question as stimulating as the racing on the track. Anyone familiar with the "bog" knows what I mean.

As I sat in the stands for my very first world class racing experience, I could hear and literally feel the rumble of those brilliantly orange-colored, Chevy V-8 powered Gulf McLarens found so often on The Glen circuit. I realized then that the racing bug must have bitten me as the likes of Dennis Hulme and Peter Revson piloted their mega-horsepowered Group 7 Can-Am race cars to victory at The Glen. It was apparent to me then that I wanted racing at The Glen and Kendall Motor Oil to play some role in my life.

Those feelings have manifested themselves as a 27 year career with Kendall, a fabulous business relationship with the people of WGI and its fans, and a love affair with speed, horsepower and the circuit carved out of farmland near Watkins Glen, New York. Kendall has entertained thousands of customers at The Glen and has made many great deals as a result of our involvement with WGI.

From Kendall's earliest involvement with Watkins Glen, when races were run through the city streets, to our current status as the official motor oil of WGI and the official partner in this year's 50th Anniversary, we have enjoyed nothing but success in everything we've done at The Glen. In the meantime, we have also enjoyed the patronage of the many fans who attend its races. Just as Winston has enjoyed a tremendous relationship with NASCAR and has certainly seen sales rise as a result of their involvement, we too have grown our business and have forged many great customer relationships through our racing partnership with WGI. What a great way to promote one's products: experiencing the thrills of racing at The Glen with a prospect, a customer, or just a friend. Thanks to all of you for helping Kendall grow its business and for thrills at every event.

Watkins Glen and I will both be 50 years old this year. Happy Birthday, Watkins Glen, and thanks for all the memories.

Sincerely

Gregory W. Booth
General Manager
Kendall Motor Oil

# A WORD *from* ZIPPO

MICHAEL SCHULER

Dear Friends and Associates at Watkins Glen International,

On behalf of Zippo Manufacturing Company, I'm pleased to extend our best wishes and hearty congratulations on the 50th anniversary celebration of road racing in the United States.

The Zippo family has long enjoyed the spectacular racing events in the beautiful Finger Lakes region. You are to be commended for providing such a high level of entertainment to so many motorsports enthusiasts for half a century. Your efforts to bring motorsports enjoyment to the entire family has created a whole new generation of racing enthusiasts.

Zippo is proud to be part of this outstanding racing heritage. While many individual family members have enjoyed events at Watkins Glen throughout the years, the Zippo sponsorship of the U.S. Vintage Grand Prix beginning in 1993 sparked the interest of the entire Zippo family of employees and associates. It is with great pleasure that we join you for our sixth year of the beautiful and exciting sport of vintage auto racing.

Again, we are proud to contribute to the presentation of the spectacular 50th anniversary celebration, and extend our good wishes for a great racing season.

Sincerely,

Michael A. Schuler
President and CEO

# INTRODUCTION

*by* JACKIE STEWART

"The hospitality, the friendliness, the intimacy of that small corner of America will never be forgotten by the true enthusiasts of motor sport."

JACKIE STEWART

Watkins Glen will always be a very special place for me.

It was the first place I ever raced at in the United States, and it was also the last place I ever drove a race car in anger. I've had the good fortune to win there, and it was also the scene of one of my greatest personal tragedies.

My first visit to The Glen was in 1965. The fact that it was my first season in Formula One added to the excitement of going to the United States to drive. I in fact finished third in the World Championship that year, driving for the BRM team along with Graham Hill. We stayed at The Glen Motor Inn, where I was first acquainted with thc Franzcsc family. Watkins Glen was an immensely hospitable small town to visit, with the beauty of the fall in full bloom. I thoroughly enjoyed my experience.

The 1968 race was a good one for me. I won the U.S. Grand Prix driving the Matra Ford, leading from start to finish. That was a very important race for me. It was in that race that I first recognized that you could actually control the pace of a race if they considered you to be the man to beat. If I went faster the whole field went faster; if I went slower, so also did the other competitors — a very good feeling. As you may recall, that was the year that Jim Clark died, and I had sort of been given the mantle of the driver to beat after Jimmy passed away. Watkins Glen was the first race I really felt comfortable at wearing that position.

**... I still have good memories of the Glen. I have returned to be a commentator for television with ABC and ESPN, so I have seen the circuit develop over the years ...**

JACKIE STEWART

In 1970 I led the Grand Prix for 82 laps in my Tyrrell Ford before a mechanical failure interrupted our day. The U.S. Grand Prix of 1971 allowed me to win the pole position and I led the early laps, but my car developed problems that would not allow me to stay up front. I had to be satisfied with slowing down and finishing fifth, although my teammate Francois Cevert, who was a great friend, went on to win.

I also had the pleasure of driving several fabulous sports cars at The Glen in Can-Am and GT racing. In 1970 I drove Jim Hall's Can-Am Chaparral called the "vacuum cleaner" with an auxiliary motor to create the first real ground effects on the race car. In 1971 I also drove for Carl Haas in a Lola T-260, where I gained pole but unfortunately ran into tire trouble as the race progressed.

I was able to win the 1972 U.S. Grand Prix, where I had secured pole position and led from start to finish. Again I was driving for Ken Tyrrell in a Tyrrell Ford. Very satisfying.

1973 was a very different picture. It should have been my 100th Grand Prix start. I had decided in April that I would retire at the end of the season, win or lose. As it happened, I secured the World Championship at the Italian Grand Prix in Monza in early September, so Watkins Glen was going to be my last race in a Formula One car. Francois Cevert was going to be number one on the team for 1974, although he never knew it. Ken Tyrrell and I had kept it a secret and in fact no one else knew that I was going to retire after that race — not even my wife, Helen, who was with me that weekend. Sadly, Francois Cevert crashed heavily during practice Saturday morning. It was an horrendous accident which took the life of a wonderfully charming, personable, handsome young man, who was a tremendous friend to both Helen and me. In respect to Francois, Ken Tyrrell and I withdrew the team, so I ended my career with 99 starts and 27 wins.

Even though that was to be my last weekend as a Grand Prix driver, I still have good memories of The Glen. I have returned to be a commentator for television with ABC and ESPN, so I have seen the circuit develop over the years, even when the Grand Prix was not being held there. Each time I have had the privilege of staying at The Glen Motor Inn.

There always has been a deep sense of charm about The Glen. The large majority of spectators were true enthusiasts of motor sports, and there always was a great atmosphere. Cameron Argetsinger, Mal Currie, John Saunders and the merry band of men and women who made Watkins Glen happen were very special people. The hospitality, the friendliness, the intimacy of that small corner of America will never be forgotten by the true enthusiasts of motor sport.

Now, I invite you to look back and enjoy some of the highlights of 50 years of racing at Watkins Glen. I think of myself as being privileged to have shared in a little part of its history.

# Racing in The Streets

## The Day They Stopped The Trains

Franklin Street — the main artery through the village of Watkins Glen, N.Y. — has been transformed to the front straightaway for the first post-World War II road race in the United States. The grid is set for the start of the first Grand Prix. On the front row are Briggs Cunningham in the BuMerc (left), joined by Mike Vaughn in his Lagonda. In the second row are George Weaver's "Lil Poison" Maserati (left), and the eventual winner, the Alfa Romeo of Frank Griswold.

Cameron Argetsinger bought a sports car in 1948, which entitled him to full membership in the Sports Car Club of America. Now all he needed was a place to race it.

Argetsinger had a dream of holding a European-style road race. A resident of Youngstown, Ohio, Argetsinger spent his summers at the family cottage on Seneca Lake in Schuyler County, in the New York Finger Lakes, and became a law student at Cornell University in nearby Ithaca. He began to fashion a circuit on the challenging roads, with a starting point at the County Court House in Watkins Glen.

Argetsinger had little precedent on which to base his dream. Very popular in Europe, sports car racing had little tradition in North America. There were a few brief successes — the Vanderbilt Cups, for instance — but both World Wars ended competition in the United States. Following the second World War, there were no plans to hold sports car races in this country. The Sports Car Club of America's main interests lay in the display and preservation of classic sports cars.

"NP" means no passing. The Sports Car Club of America created several no passing zones on the eve of the 1948 Grand Prix. Getting ready to start posting the signs are (left to right) Walt Breuhaus, David Whitcomb, Lester Smalley, Cameron Argetsinger and Bill Milliken.

But that didn't stop Argetsinger. He laid out a challenging 6.6-mile circuit, and presented his plans to the Watkins Glen Chamber of Commerce — which enthusiastically realized the potential of extending the tourist season past Labor Day. Impressed with the show of support, the SCCA helped the community get a field of cars for the event. Arrangements were made with the New York Central Railroad to "stop the trains," and on October 2, 1948, an outlandish dream became a reality.

A crowd of 10,000 cheered as Frank Griswold defeated Briggs Cunningham in a pair of races. The Glen's racing lore began that day, as Bill Milliken flipped his Bugatti at a turn known forever afterwards as "Milliken's Corner." Kentucky driver Denver Cornett rolled his MG TC into a dry stream bed after crossing the stone bridge during the four-lap Junior Prix. He emerged unhurt, and after using his spare wheel and borrowing a spare wheel from sportsman Briggs Cunningham to replace the two bent wheels, he went on to race in the Grand Prix.

Miles Collier joined the legends of The Glen the following year, when he took the "Ardent Alligator" — a highly modified Ford-powered English Riley — past Cunningham and George Roberts on the final lap to win the Grand Prix.

**(Right)** Cameron Argetsinger takes his red MG TC around Milliken's Corner during the inaugural Watkins Glen Grand Prix. For years, he dreamed of holding a European-style road race on the roads around the Finger Lakes village.

**(Lower Right)** Cameron Argetsinger at the wheel of Bill Milliken's Type 35A Bugatti, which he drove in the 1949 Grand Prix.

**(Below)** Arthur Richards, (right) writer for the Elmira Star-Gazette, was one of the first people Argetsinger contacted about the possibility of holding a race. Below, Argetsinger and Richards meet prior to the 1959 Grand Prix.

**(Bottom)** Two of The Glen's pioneers, Cameron Argetsinger and Lester Smalley, meet at Smalley's Service Station on Franklin Street in Watkins Glen, where cars were inspected over the first decade of racing. Argetsinger drove this Riley-powered Healey Silverstone in the 1950 Grand Prix.

My wife was convinced that I was going to win and that it wouldn't be fair to the other drivers and they would all go home mad.

CAMERON ARGETSINGER

Miles and his brother, Sam Collier, had founded the Automobile Racing Club of America, which held sports car races in the Thirties. Both were enthusiastic supporters of racing at Watkins Glen. Sam Collier lost his life while leading the 1950 Grand Prix, and his brother retired from racing that day.

The 1950 Grand Prix was won by Erwin Goldschmidt, and the crowds were estimated at over 100,000. However, Collier's fatal accident and another incident which injured four spectators raised questions about the feasibility of racing on public roads, with spectators literally spilling out onto the race course. The organizers took additional precautions and had a safe race in 1951, won by former short track midget driver Phil Walters over John Fitch.

# 1948 Circuit

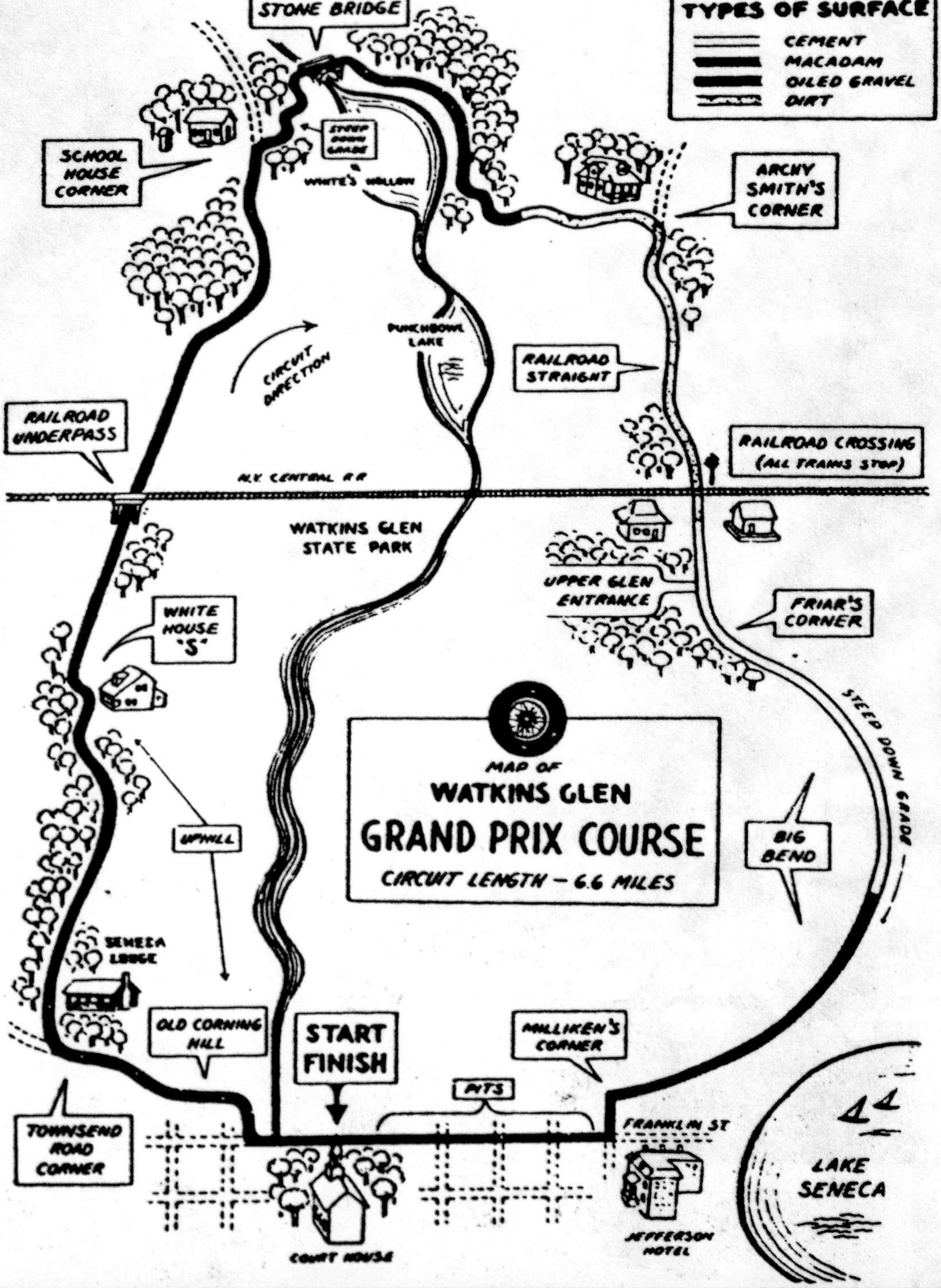


The 1948-52 circuit, as portrayed by Sam Cobean, New Yorker Artist and summer resident of Watkins Glen.

"Watkins Glen was terribly important," recalled John Fitch, who returned to The Glen to win the 1952 Seneca Cup. "It broke the ice. It established a rebirth. It was a model for all the other circuits that appeared later."

What if Watkins Glen hadn't taken the lead, would there still have been road racing?

"If they had them, it would have been much later," Fitch theorized. "The Watkins Glen race really kicked it off. It drew people from all over the country. It was a fantastic crowd. There was a real interest — almost a hunger — for this kind of thing. It just built up and built up for many years, because there hadn't been any such races. And when it happened, it drew people from everywhere."

People came from all over to see the 1952 Grand Prix, which began as a classic duel, with Briggs Cunningham taking the lead at School House Corner, and completing the first lap followed by the cars of Fitch, Fred Wacker and Walters. Suddenly, the unthinkable happened. A car brushed the crowd at the end of Franklin Street — the main artery in the village — and continued, not knowing that seven-year-old Frankie Fazzary was dead and a dozen other spectators lie injured. The race was halted, and never restarted.

**It was all very experimental and astonishing. It was a big wild adventure.**

JOHN FITCH

**(Above)** The field is set for the four- lap Junior Prix, a qualifying race for the 1948 Grand Prix. George Weaver is driving his Maserati into position in the second row.

**(Right)** Crossing the Stone Bridge, halfway around the 6.6 mile circuit, Weaver leads the field in his Grand Prix Maserati RI. It is the first lap of the Junior Prix, the first lap of competition at Watkins Glen. Briggs Cunningham is second in the BuMerc, followed by eventual winner Frank Griswold, in an Alfa Romeo 2900B.

Bill Milliken stands by the sign marking "his" corner.

**(Top Right)** Emerging with only a scraped elbow, Bill Milliken surveys the damage to his Bugatti after his flip.

**(Bottom Right)** "Milliken's Corner" is about to get its name! Bill Milliken takes his Type 35A Bugatti through "Thrill Corner" — the penultimate turn of the 6.6-mile circuit — with Haig Ksayian in close pursuit in a supercharged MG TC. Milliken lost control and flipped exiting the corner.

**(Below)** Onlookers rush to Milliken's overturned Bugatti. Milliken escaped with minor bruises, but the corner was known by his name from that time on.

**(Right)** Denver Cornett also flipped during the Junior Prix. Cornett rolled his MG TC into a dry creek bed after crossing the Stone Bridge. Cornett (alongside car) tosses his helmet after emerging unhurt from the car. The only damage was a pair of bent wheels. He used his spare tire, borrowed a wheel from sportsman Briggs Cunningham, and drove the car in the Grand Prix later in the afternoon.

**(Below Right)** Briggs Cunningham takes the BuMerc around Milliken's Corner during the inaugural Grand Prix. Cunningham finished second in both the Junior Prix and Grand Prix in this special, which married a Buick engine and chassis with a modified Mercedes-Benz SSK body. A regular at The Glen for over a decade, Cunningham never won at the circuit although he finished second in the Grand Prix in 1948, 1949 and 1950.

"Like Camelot, there was that brief, bright period when we early drivers came close to experiencing the freedom of the highway.

I sometimes wonder if road racing would have returned to this country if Cam Argetsinger hadn't spent his summer vacations in Watkins Glen, setting records through all of the various adjoining towns in his Packard."

BILL MILLIKEN

**(Top)** Frank Griswold takes the checkered flag to win the 1948 Watkins Glen Grand Prix in an Alfa Romeo 2900B.

**(Above)** Wayne, Pa., driver Frank Griswold (right) accepts the first place trophy from Watkins Glen Mayor Allen D. Erway after winning the 1948 Grand Prix.

**(Left)** Frank Griswold, second from left, and Briggs Cunningham hold their trophies after finishing one-two in both races at Watkins Glen on October 2, 1948. At left is chief starter Nils Mickelson. At right, is Smith Hempstone Oliver, curator of the Smithsonion Institution, who was the chief announcer for the inaugural event.

**(Right)** Starter Nils Mickelson waves the green flag to start the 1949 Grand Prix. In the front row are the Alfa Romeo of George Huntoon (No. 23) and the Merlin of Kenneth Hill (No. 64, popularly known as the Flying Banana); in row two are the Alfa Romeo of Mal Ord (No. 40) and the FWD-Miller of Bill Milliken (No. 26); and row three has Paul Timmins in an Ardun Special and Col. George Felton (No. 59) in the Vauxhall.

**(Center Left)** Action in turn one, entrance to Old Corning Road near the main entrance to the Gorge, during the 1949 Grand Prix. Roland Keith (49) leads a group in an HRG, as Peter Iselin (46), HRG, and Jack Pry (43), MG TC, recover from a spin.

**(Center Right)** A group of cars exit turn one and head up Old Corning Road. Peter Iselin (46), in an HRG, leads the MG TCs of David Whitcomb (19) and E. Reg Ogilvie.

**(Below Right)** The back wheels of Gus Ehrman's MG TC leave the ground after crossing the railroad tracks in the 1949 Grand Prix. He's being chased by the MG TC of Karl Brocken, who went on to finish seventh, five positions ahead of Ehrman.

**(Below)** Briggs Cunningham prior to the 1949 Grand Prix in a Ferrari 166 Inter. Standing next to the car is Alfred Momo, his crew chief and master technician. Cunningham drove the car to second place finishes in both the Seneca Cup and the Grand Prix.

**(Above)** T.H.L. "Tommy" Cole has all four wheels of his HRG off the ground during the 1949 Grand Prix. He finished fifth in the Seneca Cup and fourth in the Grand Prix, and won the B class in both races.

**(Right)** Wilbur Shaw (Right), the Grand Marshal for the 1949 Grand Prix, meets driver Ken Hill prior to the Grand Prix. At left is photographer A. Cohen. Shaw was a three-time winner of the Indianapolis 500, and at the time was president of the Indianapolis Motor Speedway.

**(Right)** Miles Collier sits in the Ardent Alligator on the shore of Lake Seneca prior to the 1949 Grand Prix.

**(Below)** Miles Collier receives the trophy for winning the 1949 Grand Prix from famed tenor James Melton, who sang for the New York Metropolitan Opera. At right is Lloyd "Rocky" Neereamer, the zone supervisor for the American Automobile Association. Collier won the race in the "Ardent Alligator," a highly-modified Ford-powered Riley, passing Briggs Cunningham and Floyd Roberts on the final lap.

Two views of the start of the 1950 Grand Prix. Note that starter Nils Mickelson is waving an American flag, signifying the race is a true international event. Tom Cole (No. 104), in a Cadillac-Allard J2, shares the front row with Bill Milliken, in a Bugatti Type 54. Fred Wacker (No. 8) is alone in the second row in a Cadillac-Allard J2. Briggs Cunningham, in a Cadillac-Healey Silverstone, is joined by J. Bruce Stevenson (No. 89) in the Meyer Special. Sam Collier is in a Ferrari 166 Inter, two cars behind Stevenson, while John Fitch's white "Fitch B Special" is three cars behind Cunningham. Eventual winner Erwin Goldschmidt's Allard J2 is all the way back at the end of the left-hand row.

**(Top)** Action in the 1950 Seneca Cup. George Weaver leads the pack in his Maserati R1 (he led races at The Glen in that car all five years the cars raced through the streets), followed by the Cadillac-Healey of Phil Walters and the Cadillac-Allard of Erwin Goldschmidt. Walters, a star on the short track midget circuit under the pseudonym Ted Tappett running his first American road race, won the event in 67.13 mph. Goldschmidt finished second in the Seneca Cup and won the Grand Prix.

**(Top Left)** Erwin Goldschmidt rounds the first turn as he begins his final lap of the 1950 Grand Prix.

**(Top Right)** Popular Sam Collier lost his life when he flipped in a Ferrari early in the 1950 Grand Prix. Collier was a founder of the Automobile Racing Club of America, which held road races prior to World War II and competed in the 1948 Watkins Glen Grand Prix.

**(Left)** Erwin Goldschmidt's Cadillac-powered Allard J2 is a blur as he takes Nils Mickelson's checkered flag in winning the 1950 Grand Prix.

**(Opposing Page)** Erwin Goldschmidt celebrates his victory in the 1950 Grand Prix, joined by his wife Madge and son Anthony.

(**Opposing Page**) George Weaver was a double winner in 1951, winning the Seneca Cup in his Maserati RI, a Grand Prix car from the Thirties. Behind the car are Barbara Weaver and Col. George Felton, a pioneer of the Automobile Racing Club of America. Weaver competed at The Glen through the early Sixties, winning many races.

(**Right**) George Weaver takes Nils Mickelson's checkered flag in winning the 1951 Queen Catharine Cup in the Jowett Javelin Jupiter.

(**Below**) Huge crowds encircled the entire 6.6-mile circuit. Here fans gather at Friar's Corner, so named after the Franciscan monks that owned the nearby posh Glen Springs resort.

H-C

**(Opposing Page)** Two of Briggs Cunningham's top drivers, Phil Walters (left) and John Fitch. Both men won races in the streets of Watkins Glen, and achieved greatness as drivers in a variety of cars and venues. Fitch became a member of the factory Mercedes-Benz team, and enjoyed a distinguished career in Europe as well as this country.

**(Top Left)** Phil Walters sweeps through the final turn into downtown Watkins Glen to win the 1951 Grand Prix in a Cunningham C-2.

**(Left)** Saxon Marsh, driving the Altemus Stabilizer Special, is about to be lapped by the 2.3-litre Ferrari of John Fitch during the 1951 Seneca Cup. Fitch finished second to the Maserati of George Weaver, in his first of two runnerup finishes that afternoon.

(Opposing Page) Bill Spear (right) after winning the 1952 Queen Catharine Cup in an OSCA. Sitting with him is noted mechanic Alfred Momo.

**(Left)** The cars are rolling for the start of the 1951 Queen Catharine Cup race. Edward Kinsley Jr. is off to a quick start in an MG TC, followed by William W. Saunders III in an MG TC and Gus Ehrman in an MG TD. The eventual winner is George Weaver, whose white No. 15 Jowett Javelin Jupiter is at the top of the photo.

**(Below)** Walter Hansgen got his first start at Watkins Glen in the 1951 Grand Prix. He follows the "Eight Ball" Allard J2 of Fred Wacker in a Jaguar XK120. Hansgen was reprimanded for "following too closely" in the race. He went on to win the Grand Prix four times.

**(Right)** Jim Kimberly drives Briggs Cunningham's Ferrari 166 Inter to a 10th place finish in the 1951 Grand Prix. Cunningham finished second in this car in the 1949 Grand Prix, while Sam Collier crashed and was killed while driving this car in the 1950 Grand Prix.

**(Below Right)** Fred Wacker sits at the wheel of his "Eight Ball" Cadillac-Allard J2 prior to finishing third in the 1950 Grand Prix. Wacker was president of the Sports Car Club of America in 1952-53.

**(Far Right)** Bill Spear takes his Ferrari to a third place finish in the 1951 Grand Prix.

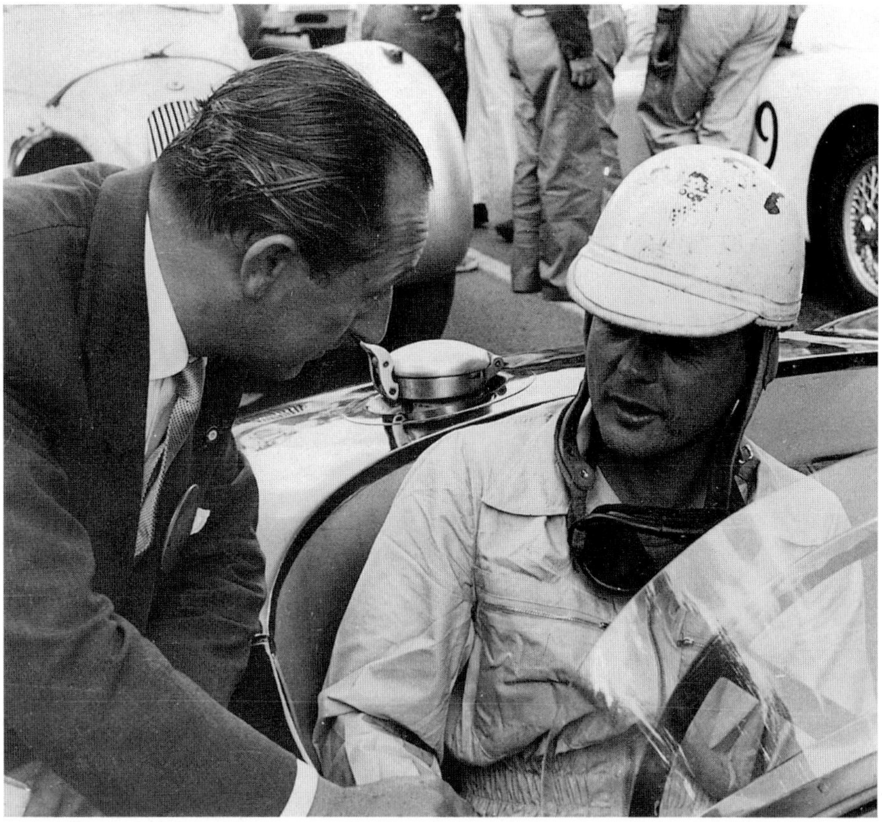

**(Left)** Phil Hill chats with Max Hoffman prior to the start of the 1952 Grand Prix. Hill, a future World Champion, had to drive the C-Type Jaguar back to California following the race!

**(Below)** Preston Gray (No. 14), driving a Cadillac-Allard, leads Irving Robbins in a Cunningham C2R near the railroad underpass during the 1952 Grand Prix.

**(Above)** The start of the 1952 Watkins Glen Grand Prix. Fred Wacker (No. 8), in a Cadillac-powered Allard, shares the front row with the No. 5 Chrysler-Allard of Joe Sabal. Briggs Cunningham (No. 53) is in the second row with the Cadillac-Allard J2 of George Harris, while John Fitch, in a Cunningham C4R, is in row three with Chrysler-Allard driver John Negley.

**(Right)** The middle of the pack gets underway for the 1952 Grand Prix. Cars visible include Art Iselin Jr. (No. 116), Traver McKenna (No. 12), Allan Patterson (No. 127), and Sherwood Johnston (No. 29).

(Opposing Page) Briggs Cunningham prior to the 1952 Grand Prix. A second place finisher at The Glen three times, Cunningham was leading the final street race at The Glen when it was red flagged. One of America's greatest sportsmen, Cunningham successfully defended the America's Cup, skippering his yacht Columbia.

(Above) The 1952 Grand Prix was preceded by three "practice laps." With the front row already on their way up Old Corning Road, Briggs Cunningham (left) in the No. 53 Cunningham C4R and George Harris negotiate turn one.

(Right) Briggs Cunningham takes the lead in the 1952 race in his Cunningham C4R.

**(Above)** The final lap of racing in downtown Watkins Glen. Briggs Cunningham leads at the end of the first lap of the 1952 Grand Prix down Franklin Street, followed by teammate John Fitch. Moments later, Fred Wacker, driving the third place Allard, attempted to pass Fitch prior to the first turn. Wacker brushed the crowd, killing seven-year-old Frankie Fazzary and injuring 12 other spectators. The race was halted and never restarted.

**(Far Left)** Fred Wacker (left) talks with noted opera tenor James Melton prior to the start of the 1952 Grand Prix. Melton took the microphone after the accident at the conclusion of the first lap, and sang "God Bless America" and "Ave Maria" to calm the crowd.

**(Left)** John Duval was the Watkins Glen announcer during the 1952 Grand Prix. He kept the crowd calm after the Grand Prix accident. Duval, with his dry wit and precise pronounciation, became a fixture at Watkins Glen, continuing his announcing duties into the Seventies.

# Years of Transition

## The Glen Finds a Home

There was a loud national outcry to stop the races following the tragic 1952 Grand Prix. But the majority of the Watkins Glen area community rallied to keep the races.

Over the next eight years, several major obstacles were placed in their path, but the determined community pulled together and successfully hurdled each one. By the beginning of the next decade, Watkins Glen was able to take its place as one of the major international road racing circuits.

Originally, the Watkins Glen Grand Prix committee planned a major overhaul of the 6.6-mile street circuit, moving the start/finish line to the railroad straight near the upper entrance of the Watkins Glen State Park and taking steps to place all spectators at least 75 feet from the circuit wherever possible. A bill which would have outlawed street racing in New York passed the New York State Senate, but was defeated in the Assembly. Suddenly, plans ground to a halt on April 21, 1953 — less than five months from the planned race date — when Lloyds of London refused to insure the event if it took place on its present course.

The committee acted quickly in a search for an alternative track. One in the Town of Orange was ruled out by conservationists. Finally, after inspecting five possible sites, on June 24, Watkins Glen attorney

**The field for the Seneca Cup streaks by after taking the green flag from lavender-suited Tex Hopkins in 1956 action, the first racing at the first permanent circuit at The Glen.**

One of the legendary races at The Glen was the duel between Paul O'Shea and Bob Holbert at the 1957 Glen Classic. Holbert won the preliminary race, but O'Shea, in a Mercedes-Benz 300SL, came back to win the feature after a nose-to-tail battle with Holbert's Porsche RS. Both drivers are still side-by-side and smiling on the victory lap. O'Shea holds the checkered flag, while Holbert is joined by his wife and young son, Al Holbert, who would become one of The Glen's greatest drivers.

Henry Valent outlined a 4.6-mile circuit adjoining his family's farm in the Town of Dix, five miles southwest of Watkins Glen. In six weeks, the circuit was ready for the race, although the SCCA refused to sanction the event — feeling that the track would not be ready in time.

For three years, competition took place on the rectangular 4.6-mile circuit consisting of renovated country roads which were shut down for one weekend each year. Phil Walters called it "a course for brave men." He obviously fit into that category, following up his 1951 downtown victory with a victory in the 1954 Grand Prix in a Cunningham C4R. Dr. M.R.J. Wyllie, an engineer for Gulf Oil Corporation, also fit that description, winning the Seneca Cup race from 1953 through 1955.

Ultimately, the temporary nature of this circuit rendered it impractical. A hard winter, heavy summer rains — followed by several days of use by heavy farm vehicles just prior to the event — caused problems in 1955, when the fresh pavement began to break up during the race weekend.

Early in 1956, the SCCA made several monetary demands of the Watkins Glen Grand Prix Corporation, which announced on May 7 that the races would go on, using the same course, but without SCCA sanction. But in July, the corporation took a new approach, announcing the purchase of 580 acres of land — including some of the area used in the 4.6-mile circuit — and plans to build a 2.3-mile permanent circuit. The Schuyler County community rallied by "waving the green flag" to fund the $50,000 circuit. The track was designed to simulate the original street course, with long straights and fast corners.

**(Above)** The field is on the grid and ready for the start of the 1953 Seneca Cup race, the first event on the second Watkins Glen course. Dr. M.R.J. Wyllie (No. 27) won the race, starting a three-year winning streak in the event. Cameron Argetsinger, in Jaguar No. 22, finished fifth after losing his brakes while running third. Both Wyllie and Argetsinger drove the Jaguar XK120M.

**(Far Left)** A car swings wide in the final turn during the 1953 Grand Prix. This corner is the site of the current Gate Three entrance to Watkins Glen International.

**(Left)** Walt Hansgen, in the No. 10 Hansgen Jaguar Special, leads the Cadillac-Allard J-2 of George Harris III off the final corner during the 1953 Grand Prix. The pair exchanged the lead at least five times on that final lap. This was the first of Hansgen's many victories at The Glen.

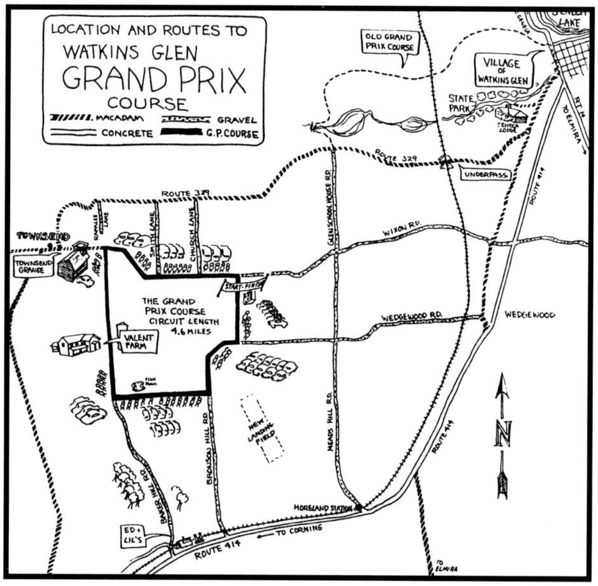


**(Above)** The 1953-55 Watkins Glen Circuit.

**(Below)** Gordon MacKensie heads down the current County Route 16 towards the final turn during the 1953 Grand Prix. This photo was taken from the site of the current WGI Registration and Ticket offices. Second is Charles Limbacher, in an MG TD.

*continued from page 38*

The course was completed on the night before opening practice for the 1956 Grand Prix. Competitors in opening practice found the surface "green," with cars sustaining damage from flying stones. On the eve of the race, the SCCA and Road Racing Driver's Club issued telegrams urging the drivers and officials to withdraw in recognition of the hazards to safety and for the welfare of the sport.

Dramatically, the SCCA representative — none other than Dr. M.R.J. Wyllie — read the telegrams to the assembled group of drivers prior to the race. "How many besides myself won't race here today? Raise your hands!" Wyllie demanded. His request was met with silence, and then applause, as not a single hand was raised. The races went on, and Wyllie himself even competed, placing second in his race.

The following year, the course was cured, and The Glen hosted three weekends of racing, including the first professional race at Watkins Glen, a NASCAR Grand National event won by Buck Baker.

For 1958, The Glen took the next big step, hosting a professional sports car race. It's fitting that Cameron Argetsinger, the founder of racing at Watkins Glen and now the Grand Prix Corporation's Executive Director, would take that step, known by some at the time as "Argetsinger's folly."

The race was called Formula Libre (free formula), or more liberally translated, "run what you brung" — Formula One cars, sports cars, even circle

**(Right)** Officials for the 1954 Grand Prix included (left to right) Capt. George E. T. Eyston, chief steward; Nils Mickelson, chief starter; and George Rand, of the race competition committee.

**(Below Right)** The network of roads that comprised the new 4.6 mile circuit included Townsend Corner, shown here during the 1955 Collier Brothers Memorial Trophy race.

track midgets. Joakim Bonnier of Sweden won the inaugural Formula Libre race in a Grand Prix car identical to the Maserati driven to the previous year's World Championship by the great Juan Manuel Fangio. Bonnier had to work for that victory, holding off the Ferraris of Americans Phil Hill and Dan Gurney, who eventually finished second.

Over the next two years, the number and quality of international entries increased. Popular Stirling Moss, "the uncrowned champion" of Formula One racing, won both times. The 1960 race had a standout field, including reigning World Champion Jack Brabham.

While actual Formula One racing came to America in 1959 and 1960, neither the race at Sebring, Florida, nor the event at Riverside, California, was successful. On August 28, 1961 Cameron Argetsinger was given the go-ahead for Watkins Glen to host the United States Grand Prix, just over one month away.

Thirteen years after seeing his dream of racing on the streets of Watkins Glen come to life, Argetsinger was able to realize a bigger dream. The full attention of the international racing community was focused on The Glen.

**(Above)** Start of the first Collier Brothers Memorial Trophy Race. On the front row are Leech Cracraft (No. 208) in an MG TF, flanked by the MG TD of Milton Cooper.

**(Right)** The paddock as it looked in 1953. George Weaver's Maserati RI (No. 4) is at the far left. Note the Hughey farm in the background — it's still a familiar site to fans at the Watkins Glen races today.

**(Opposing Page)** Gus Ehrman wears the winner's laurels after capturing the 1954 Collier Brothers Memorial in an MG TD.

**(Left)** 1954 was the first year Briggs Cunningham's team raced on the 4.6 mile circuit. Phil Walters takes the checkered flag in a Cunningham C4R, becoming the first two-time winner of the Sports Car Grand Prix.

**(Bottom Left)** Oakleigh Robinson takes the checkered flag after winning the 1955 Collier Brothers Memorial, in an MG TF.

**(Left)** Sherwood Johnston drives to victory in the 1955 Grand Prix, in a D-Type Jaguar owned by Briggs Cunningham.

**(Below)** Sherwood Johnston is about to start his victory lap after winning the 1955 Grand Prix, the final race on the 4.6-mile circuit.

**(Right)** George Weaver (left) receives the trophy for winning the 1956 Seneca Cup from Gene Osborne. It was Weaver's fourth victory at The Glen, coming in a new Maserati 4CLT.

**(Below Right)** Under very different working conditions than today, Charles Schott works on his Jaguar beside Smalley's Garage prior to technical inspection.

**(Below)** Smalley's Garage in downtown Watkins Glen was home of the safety and technical inspection from 1949 through 1961. Smalley's Garage is still in operation today and looks much the same as it did in this 1954 photo.

**(Above)** Three of The Glen's pioneers celebrate the 10th anniversary at the 1958 Grand Prix while admiring the engine of a Ferrari. Left to right are noted cartoonist Charles Addams, '48 winner Frank Griswold, competitor-official-engineer Bill Milliken and Thomas Schatchard.

**(Right)** Walt Hansgen takes the laurel wreath and is about to get his (paper!) cup of champagne after winning the 1957 Sports Car Grand Prix. At the right is his mechanic, Alfred Momo.

**(Opposing Page)** William Sadler was a strong supporter of racing at The Glen, competing in "Sadler Specials." The Canadian defied an SCCA ban on racing at The Glen to win the 1956 Glen Classic.

**(Right)** Racer/journalist Denise McCluggage prepares for the start of a race in a North American Racing Team OSCA Formula Jr. She won a 1957 Ladies Race at The Glen, driving a Porsche 550RS.

**(Below Right)** Hal Ullrich drives the Excalibur J to a third place finish in the 1953 Grand Prix. The photo was taken at the corner of Hedden and Baker Hill Roads.

(**Above**) Dr. M.R.J. Wyllie wears the laurel wreath after winning the 1953 Seneca Cup in a Jaguar XK120M, his first of three consecutive Seneca Cup victories. He is joined by his wife, Peggy, who won a pair of Ladies Races at The Glen in the late Fifties.

(**Right**) Walt Hansgen is joined by master mechanic Alfred Momo after winning the 1959 Grand Prix in a Lister-Jaguar.

**(Right)** In the heat of the battle, the memorable 1957 Glen Classic rages with Paul O'Shea leading Bob Holbert out of Turn One. The racing was so close, that both drivers shared the lap record at that time.

**(Below Right)** As cars climb the hill at the start of the 1959 Sports Car Grand Prix, other teams prepare in the paddock area. Most teams hauled their race cars behind their family vehicles, while the "high dollar" teams like Roosevelt Racing (Franklin Delano Roosevelt's son), brought their cars on double deck, multi-car open trailers.

**(Left)** "Big Jake," Bob Bucher is on his way to winning the 1957 Seneca Cup race in a Cadillac-powered Allard J2R.

**(Below Left)** Bob Bucher en route to winning the 1957 Collier Brothers Memorial race in an MGA owned by Spanky Smith. The car has been restored and is driven in Vintage competition by Joe Tierno.

**(Above)** Colorful starter Tex Hopkins surveys the front row for the 1958 Grand Prix. Ed Crawford won over teammate Walter Hansgen, as the Briggs Cunningham-owned Lister-Jaguars finished one-two.

**(Right)** Walt Hansgen dominated the 1960 Grand Prix in this new "Birdcage" Maserati Type 61, from the Cunningham stable, but dropped out with overheating problems.

**(Far Right)** Walt Hansgen signs an autograph prior to the 1960 Grand Prix. Note the framework of his Maserati, which gave it the nickname "Birdcage."

Roger Penske wears a laurel wreath after winning the E Modified class in the 1960 Sports Car Grand Prix. His Porsche RS finished second overall to Augie Pabst in the Scarab.

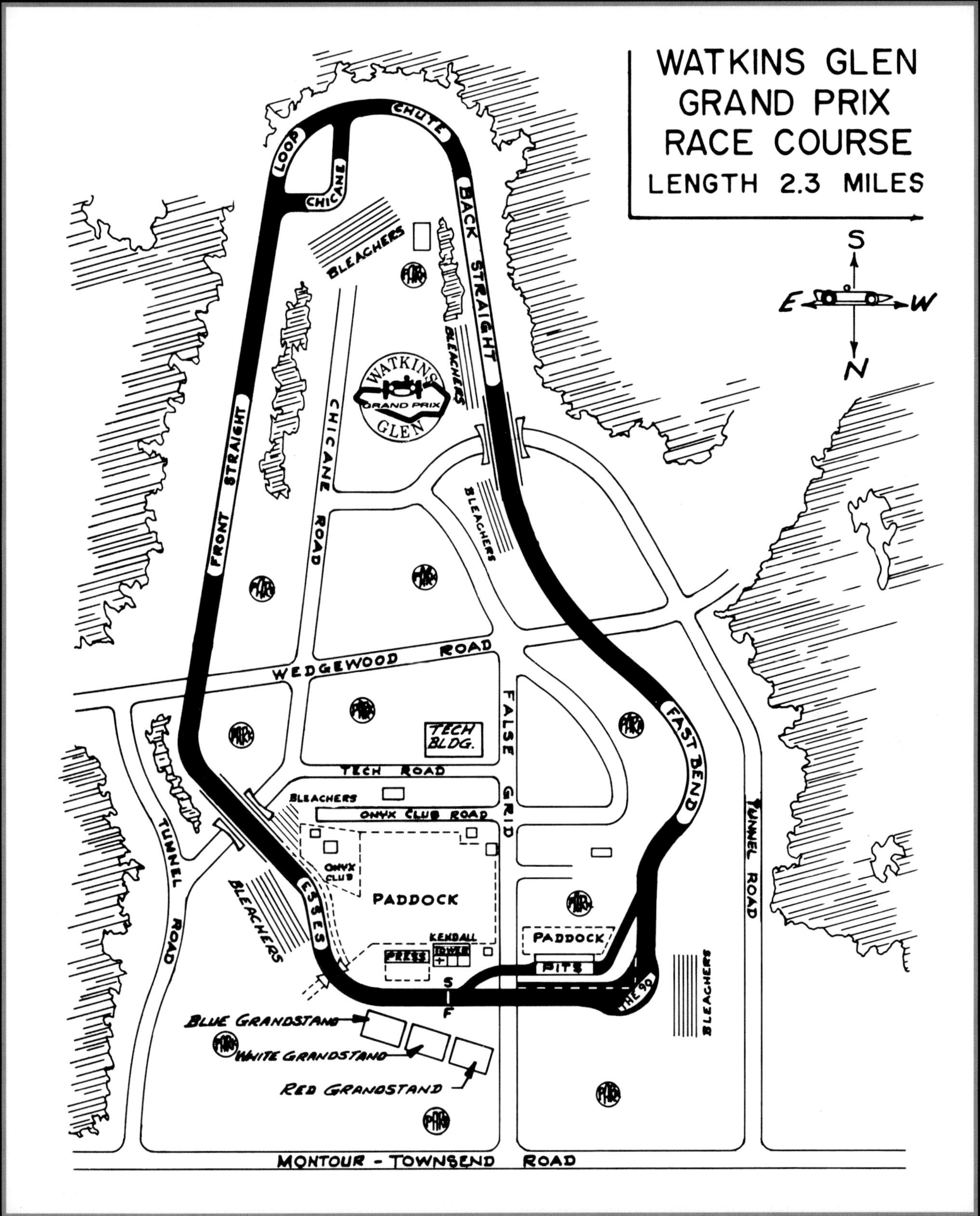


The first permanent race course at Watkins Glen, used from 1956 through 1970.

140

51
B.M

206
23

2
GM

**(Opposing Page)**
(Top) Holbert was running a strong second in the 1960 Grand Prix in a new Porsche RSK 60, but dropped out two laps from the finish with a cracked fuel tank. (Middle Left) Harry Heuer finished third in the 1960 Grand Prix in a Scarab. (Middle Right) Denise McCluggage took fifth in the 1960 Seneca Cup in an OSCA. (Bottom) Dr. M.R.J. Wyllie drives to victory in the 1960 Queen Catharine Cup.

**(Right)** Augie Pabst won the 1960 Sports Car Grand Prix in this Scarab.

**(Below)** The field is nose-to-tail in the 1960 Seneca Cup, the oldest named race in the U.S. at that time. Walt Hansgen driving a Cunningham Cooper, is tucked in right behind leader Dick Cosgrove in a Tarashi. Hansgen would go on to win the event.

**(Left)** Phil Hill is ready to drive this Ferrari in the 1958 Formula Libre race. At upper right is Dan Gurney, standing next to his Ferrari, which is ahead of the Aston-Martin DBR-300 of George Constantine and the Formula One Maserati 250F of Joakim Bonnier. Hill gave Bonnier a run for his money before breaking a prop shaft. Gurney went on to place second.

**(Center Left)** Race organizer Cameron Argetsinger (center, joined by his wife Jean) was limited by budget in the number of European teams he could invite to the Formula Libre races. But he chose wisely. Here, he is with Sweden's Joakim Bonnier prior to his victory in the 1958 race. Over the next two years, invited guests included Stirling Moss and Jack Brabham, gaining prestige and international exposure for the circuit. When the opportunity came for The Glen to host the U.S. Grand Prix in 1961, Argetsinger was ready to take that step.

**(Bottom Left)** Bob Said drove a Sadler Chevy in the 1958 Formula Libre race.

(**Above**) Stirling Moss in action. He won both the 1959 and 1960 Formula Libre races at The Glen. The dominant driver of his era, he never won the World Championship.

(**Right**) Popular Englishman Stirling Moss looks over his Coventry Climax-powered Formula One Lotus prior to driving it to victory in the 1960 Formula Libre race. At right is car owner Rob Walker. Moss continued to visit The Glen after his driving career was cut short due to injuries suffered at Goodwood Circuit in England in 1962.

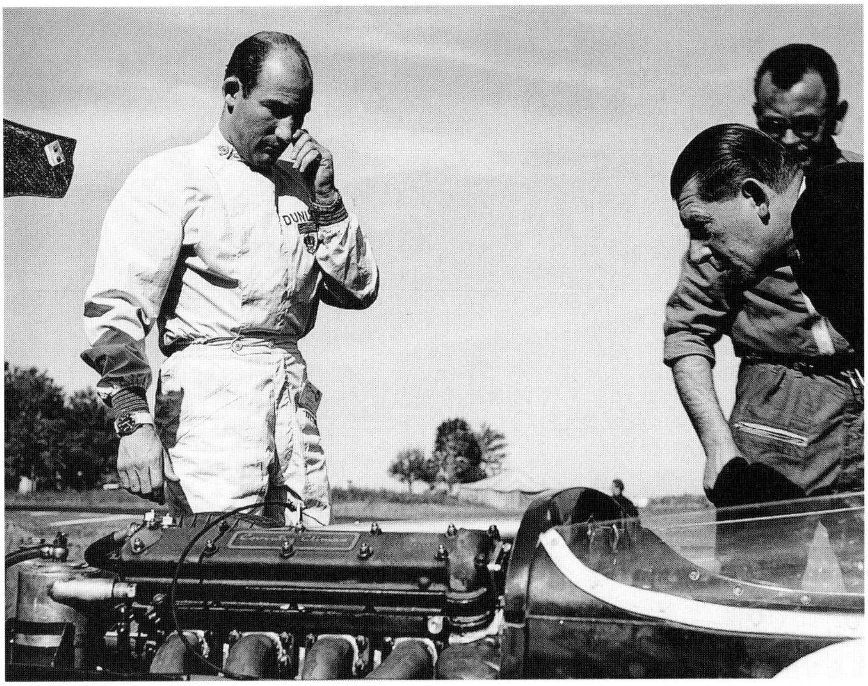

**(Above Right)** Bonnier prepares in his Yeoman Credit Cooper for the 1960 Formula Libre, under the watchful eye of eventual winner Stirling Moss.

**(Right)** After winning the 1958 Formula Libre race at The Glen, Joakim Bonnier returned for another Formula Libre race, 10 U.S. Grands Prix and many Six Hour and Can-Am races.

**(Top)** Paul O'Shea leans on the D Jaguar he drove in the 1960 Formula Libre race. He was hired to drive by David Murray, owner of the European Ecurie Ecosse team. Wilkie Wilkinson is the mechanic in the photo.

**(Left)** 1959 LeMans winner Roy Salvadori finished third in the 1960 Formula Libre, driving a Cooper-Monaco for David Murray's Ecurie Ecosse team.

**(Below)** One of the greatest drivers of all time, Stirling Moss on his way to victory in the 1959 Formula Libre race.

**(Top)** 1959 and 1960 World Champion Jack Brabham finished second in the 1960 Formula Libre race, driving a Cooper-Climax. Brabham also won the 1966 World Championship.

**(Above)** Jack Brabham poses with a mechanic prior to the start.

**(Left)** Popular Canadian Bill Sadler drove a "Sadler Special" Corvette in the 1960 Formula Libre race.

# The Formula One Years

## The World Comes to Watkins Glen

Back in 1948, when final plans were being made for the first race through the streets of Watkins Glen, community leaders wanted to title the event "The American Grand Prix."

"No, we'll call it the Watkins Glen Sports Car Grand Prix," said Cameron Argetsinger, the law student whose dream of holding a European-style road race through the village was about to become reality.

Argetsinger then prophesied, "One day we'll have the American Grand Prix."

Argetsinger's dream took a step closer to reality in 1958 with the first of three Formula Libre races. Grand Prix stars, including Joakim Bonnier, Stirling Moss and Jack Brabham, and several of Europe's top sports car teams challenged America's top drivers, including Dan Gurney, Phil Hill and Bob Holbert.

The Formula One series, meanwhile, came to the United States for the first time in 1959, racing at Sebring, Florida, and ran at Riverside, California, the following year. Neither race was financially successful.

A number of venues were considered for the 1961 Grand Prix. On August 28 — only a few weeks prior to the October 8 race date — Watkins Glen was awarded the U.S. Grand Prix. The race was successful from both an artistic and a financial perspective and created the first real foothold for true Grand Prix racing in the United States.

Graham Hill roars into the lead in the No.1 BRM as Tex Hopkins waves the green flag for the start of the 1963 U.S. Grand Prix. Behind Hill are John Surtees in a Ferrari, Jack Brabham in a Brabham, Dan Gurney in a Brabham, and Richie Ginther in the No. 2 BRM.

**The start of the 1967 U.S. Grand Prix.**

Innes Ireland drove a patient race to win the inaugural F-1 race at The Glen. Finishing second was American driver Dan Gurney.

"I thought it was terrific, running the Grand Prix at Watkins Glen," Gurney recalled. "I think the Europeans looked forward to coming over for the race. At that time of year the tree colors in the surrounding territory is so fantastic, and I loved the idea of housing the cars in the garages downtown and driving them up to the track. The whole town really got into it, I know that.

"You bet it made me proud to be an American," Gurney continued. "Racing at The Glen was a special feeling. Of course, The Glen people had the courage to step up and go for it, and it worked out. It was a real fixture on our schedule."

From 1962 through 1967, Jimmy Clark and Graham Hill dominated the U.S. Grand Prix. Clark won in 1962, and then struggled with bad luck as Hill reeled off three consecutive victories. Clark won in 1966, and repeated the following year in his last visit to The Glen.

From 1968 on, the racing was anything but predictable. Mario Andretti won the pole position for the 1968 U.S. Grand Prix, in only his first race in a Formula One car.

Jackie Stewart went on to win the 1968 race while Jochen Rindt scored his first Grand Prix victory at The Glen in 1969. Another upset was in the works in 1970 when Emerson Fittipaldi triumphed in only his fourth Grand Prix.

"Watkins Glen was the beginning of my Grand Prix career," recalled

Fittipaldi with a smile. "It was a very important win, my first win, and I have great memories of Watkins Glen. I love the place, I love the people. I had a lot of fun, every time I went there."

The Glen circuit was revised to its present configuration in 1971, and for the third consecutive year, the race had a first time winner. Francois Cevert won the race for Tyrrell. His teammate Stewart repeated in 1972, while Ronnie Peterson captured the 1973 event.

The World Championship was on the line for the 1974 race, with three drivers fighting for the coveted title. Fittipaldi won the crown with a fourth place finish, beating out Clay Regazzoni and Jody Scheckter in a race won by Carlos Reutemann.

"The 1974 race was another important part of my career," Fittipaldi said. "I remember starting side by side with Clay Regazzoni, being exactly the same in the points, in the last race of the season. Again, there was tremendous pressure. It was a different kind of pressure than 1970, but it was a lot of pressure."

Over the following years, Niki Lauda, James Hunt, Gilles Villeneuve and Alan Jones would add their names to the list of Grand Prix winners at The Glen. While the crowds flocked to The Glen each October, the Grand Prix Corporation's status grew more and more uncertain. Finally unable to pay off all its debts following the 1980 event, the 1981 Grand Prix was cancelled. Racing at Watkins Glen would return in a few years, and the circuit would regain its position as America's leading road circuit, but the end of the Grand Prix signalled the end of an exciting era in American motorsports.

"To me, Watkins Glen is one of the sacred venues here in the United States," Andretti explained. "If you're going to name the traditional events, the traditional tracks, the tracks that hosted some of the big races we all remember, Watkins Glen fits that category, along with Daytona, Indianapolis, and not too many others. Watkins Glen has always been very close and dear to my heart, no question about it."

**(Left)** The United States Grand Prix finds its true home as The Glen hosts its first Grand Prix in 1961. Here Jack Brabham leads Stirling Moss, Graham Hill, Bruce McLaren, eventual winner Innes Ireland, Dan Gurney, and Jim Clark into the uphill Esses.

**(Lower Left)** Stirling Moss — The "Uncrowned" World Champion and a perennial favorite at The Glen. Moss won the 1959 and 1960 Formula Libre races, and was leading the 1961 Grand Prix when he retired with engine bearing failure.

**(Lower Right)** Jack Brabham won the pole for The Glen's inaugural U.S. Grand Prix, but retired from the race with a water leak while running second in a Cooper-Climax.

**(Bottom Right)** While Stirling Moss tested this new V-8-powered Lotus Climax for the 1961 U.S. Grand Prix, he decided to race with his proven four-cylinder engine. He was leading when he retired after 58 laps with engine bearing failure.

"I enjoyed myself racing at Watkins Glen. It was a lovely circuit to drive on, and I enjoyed it very much. It was a wonderful circuit. It's a pity they couldn't have continued to hold the Grand Prix, because it was a very enjoyable place to come to, the organization was very good, and all the Grand Prix drivers used to enjoy coming there. The track was extremely good in those days. When we raced there, it was as good as any circuit we raced on."

JACK BRABHAM

Jack Brabham's best finish in the U.S. Grand Prix was third in 1965, although the Australian placed second behind Stirling Moss in the 1960 Formula Libre race. His son, Geoff Brabham, was a two-time winner in IMSA competition at The Glen.

**(Right)** Two of America's top Grand Prix drivers of the Sixties, Richie Ginther (left) and Phil Hill, prior to the 1962 U.S. Grand Prix. Ginther ran third before retiring on lap 34 with an oil leak in his BRM. Hill, the 1961 World Champion, was rideless for the '62 event.

**(Below)** Cars exit the pits during practice for the 1961 Grand Prix. USAC short track star Lloyd Ruby is at the wheel of the privately-entered No. 26 Lotus, followed by Team Lotus driver Jimmy Clark.

**(Opposing Page)** Innes Ireland of Scotland won the first U.S. Grand Prix at The Glen, driving a Lotus. On a day of firsts, it was the first-ever Grand Prix win for both Innes and Team Lotus.

**(Above)** Dan Gurney relaxes while his crew works on his Porsche 804 prior to the 1962 Grand Prix. He went on to finish fifth.

**(Right)** Roger Penske finished ninth in the 1962 U.S. Grand Prix, his second and final Formula One start. He's driving the Dupont Zerex Anti-Freeze Lotus, one of the first "sponsored" Grand Prix cars.

**(Opposing Page)** Dan Gurney — one of the most successful Americans to complete in Grand Prix racing — in his Eagle during practice for the 1967 U.S. Grand Prix.

"It's always been a little bit of a time machine. A lot of The Glen has been there for a long time, and therefore there's a lot of tradition and memories and history involved. As you get older, it's pretty special to be able to touch that every once in a while. The fall colors were also a big part of it, but the fact that it was the Grand Prix meant a lot to us, it was like a big magnet at a certain time of year, where everybody goes."

DAN GURNEY

**(Top)** Graham Hill driving a BRM to victory in the 1964 U.S. Grand Prix.

**(Center)** John Surtees seemed headed to victory in the 1963 U.S. Grand Prix in a Ferrari 156, only to lose power with 30 laps remaining.

**(Below)** Graham Hill leads the Ferrari of John Surtees during the 1963 U.S. Grand Prix. Hill won his first of three consecutive U.S. Grands Prix in a BRM.

**(Opposing Page)** Jimmy Clark wears the laurel wreath after winning the 1962 U.S. Grand Prix in a Lotus. Clark was a three time Watkins Glen winner. The Scotsman won again in 1966 and '67, the latter only nine months before his death on April 2, 1968, in a Formula 2 race at Hockenheim, Germany.

(Above) The field is off for the 1964 U.S. Grand Prix. Out front (left to right) are Jim Clark (No. 1, Lotus), Dan Gurney (No. 6, Brabham), John Surtees (No. 7, Ferrari), and eventual winner Graham Hill (No. 3, BRM). Just behind are Mike Spence (No. 2, Lotus) and Lorenzo Bandini (No. 8, Ferrari). Leading the third wave are Bruce McLaren (No. 9, Cooper), Jack Brabham (No. 5, Brabham), and Innes Ireland (No. 11, BRP).

(Right) Cameron Argetsinger (center) accepts the 1965 Grand Prix Drivers Association award for the best organized Grand Prix in the world from Joakim Bonnier (left) and Graham Hill in London.

**(Top)** Dan Gurney, driving the No. 10 Porsche, leads the No.21 Cooper-Climax of Bruce McLaren during the 1962 U.S. Grand Prix. McLaren finished third, two positions ahead of Gurney.

**(Left)** John Surtees finished third in the 1966 U.S. Grand Prix, driving a Cooper-Maserati. Surtees repeatedly broke the lap record after pitting due to being forced off early in the race.

**(Above)** The field is set for the start of the 1965 U.S. Grand Prix. Left to right are Lorenzo Bandini (Ferrari No. 2), pole sitter and eventual winner Graham Hill (BRM No. 3), Jack Brabham (Brabham No. 7), Richie Ginther (Honda No. 11), Jackie Stewart (BRM No. 4), Jimmy Clark (Lotus No. 5), Dan Gurney (Brabham), and Mike Spence (Lotus No. 6).

**(Left)** The field completes the second lap of the 1965 U.S. Grand Prix. Graham Hill leads Jimmy Clark, Jackie Stewart, Lorenzo Bandini, Mike Spence, Jack Brabham, Dan Gurney, Richie Ginther and Joakim Bonnier.

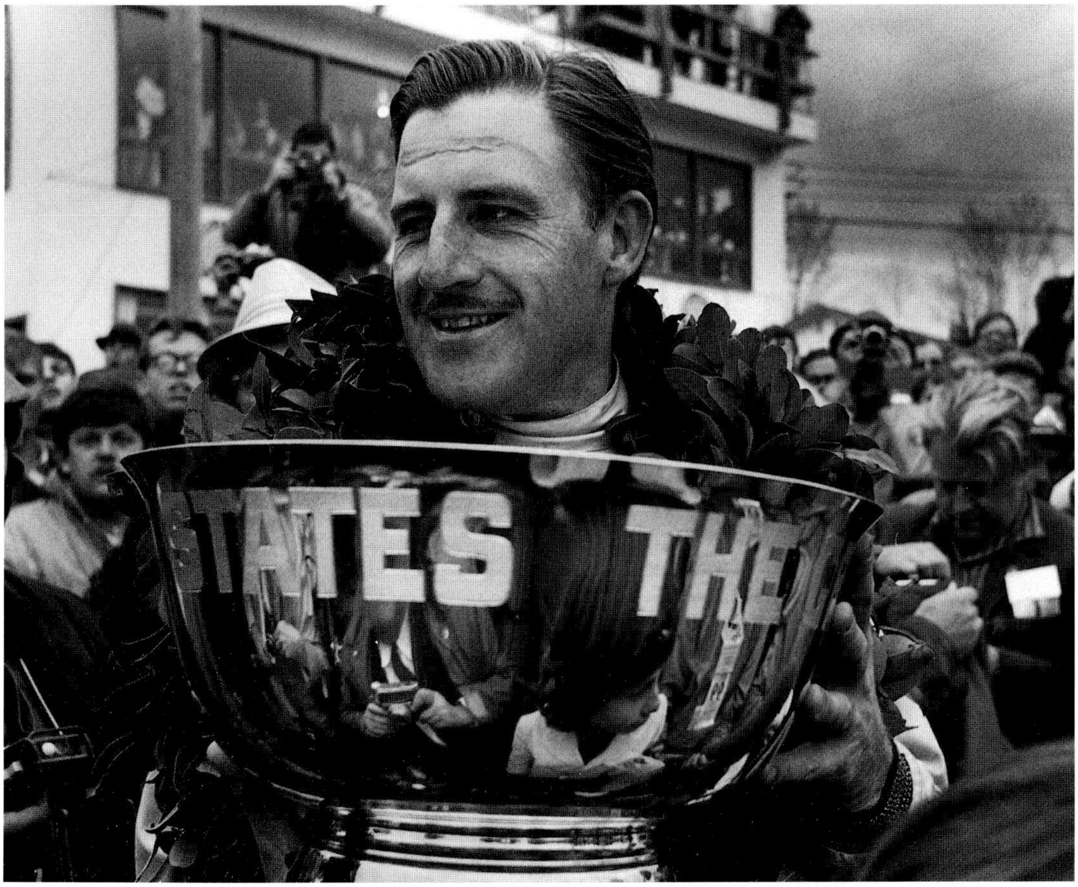


**(Left)** Graham Hill accepts the victor's cup for winning the 1965 U.S. Grand Prix in a BRM, his third consecutive U.S. Grand Prix victory.

**(Below)** Lorenzo Bandini, driving a Ferrari, leads the Lotus of Jim Clark and the Brabham of Jack Brabham during the 1966 U.S. Grand Prix.

**(Above)** Jackie Stewart qualified on the third row for the 1966 U.S. Grand Prix. He retired the Owen BRM with engine problems.

**(Top Right)** A pensive Dan Gurney awaits the 1966 race.

**(Center Right)** Bob Bondurant was part of a two-car Anglo-American Eagle entry in 1966. However, both cars retired in the early going. Bob Bondurant talks with Dan Gurney and team manager Bill Dunne (kneeling) in the pits during practice.

**(Below Right)** Denis Hulme made his Watkins Glen debut in the 1966 U.S. Grand Prix, driving for Team Brabham. He retired after 18 laps, losing oil pressure.

**(Top)** With the engines fired up, starter Tex Hopkins surveys the field seconds before doing his famous "hop" and waving the green flag to start the 1966 U.S. Grand Prix. Left to right are pole winner Jack Brabham (Brabham No. 5), Lorenzo Bandini (Ferrari No. 9), and eventual winner Jimmy Clark (Lotus No. 1).

**(Left)** After experiencing engine failure in practice, the Lotus team borrowed an engine from BRM — and Jimmy Clark drove it to victory in the 1966 U.S. Grand Prix. Ironically, this was the only Formula One victory for the BRM H-16 engine.

The field heads up the Esses during the 1967 U.S. Grand Prix.

Take the VC10
Only one airline

**(Above)** Jimmy Clark finished up a winner at Watkins Glen, winning the 1966 and 1967 U.S. Grands Prix. Left to right are Linda Eldridge of Bath, N.Y., Miss Grand Prix; Clark; Keith Duckworth of Cosworth; and Colin Chapman of Lotus.

**(Left)** Colin Chapman — seven-time winner at The Glen and leader of Team Lotus.

**(Left)** Dan Gurney is the center of attention as he drives his Westlake V12-powered Eagle from the garage during practice for the 1967 Grand Prix. Earlier in the season, Gurney won the Belgian Grand Prix at Spa-Franchorchamps, to become the first American to win a European Grand Prix in an American chassis in the modern era.

**(Below)** Dan Gurney leads the Brabham of Denis Hulme during the 1967 Grand Prix.

**(Top)** 1967 action sees Graham Hill's Lotus leading team-mate (and eventual winner) Jimmy Clark, Dan Gurney's Eagle and Jack Brabham's Brabham.

**(Right)** Three time U.S. Grand Prix winner and two time World Champion Jim Clark.

**(Top)** Denis Hulme, carrying the No. 1 of the defending World Champion, in 1968 U.S. Grand Prix action in his McLaren.

**(Left)** Dan Gurney (left), driving a McLaren, passes the Honda of John Surtees during the 1968 U.S. Grand Prix. Surtees regained the position on the final lap to finish third behind Jackie Stewart and Graham Hill, with Gurney fourth.

**(Left)** American hopefuls Mario Andretti (left) and Bobby Unser chat prior to their Formula One debuts in the 1968 U.S. Grand Prix. Andretti put his Gold Leaf Team Lotus on the pole, but the future World Champion retired with clutch trouble. Unser, a three-time Indianapolis 500 winner, went out with a blown engine in his lone Grand Prix start.

**(Below)** Jochen Rindt in the cockpit of the Gold Leaf Eagle prior to winning the 1969 U.S. Grand Prix from the pole.

**(Opposing Page)** Mario Andretti — winner of the pole position in his first start in Formula One racing.

The memories of 1968 are fantastic, because I put that car on the pole, that was my official debut in a Formula One car.

"It's a milestone in my career. Certainly, the odds against that happening are incredible. Somehow, the car was obviously good, the Lotus 49 was the fantastic car of the moment, but I was the third man on the team. Something worked out for me. We hit on a good setup, and I was just flat out, and the thing responded the way I was hoping."

MARIO ANDRETTI

**(Right)** Bruce McLaren in the cockpit of his famed orange McLaren-Cosworth. McLaren blew an engine in warmups and did not start. McLaren introduced his own car to Grand Prix racing in 1966. His teams would later enjoy success in both Can-Am and Indy cars.

**(Below)** Jochen Rindt shadows Jackie Stewart en route to winning the 1969 U.S. Grand Prix. Stewart retired his Matra with engine trouble. Despite having very different personalities, the rivals were best of friends away from the track.

**(Opposing Page)**
Jackie Stewart waits in the pits prior to the 1969 U.S. Grand Prix. Flag-to-flag winner of the '68 event, his luck soured in '69, losing oil pressure after 36 laps while running in second position.

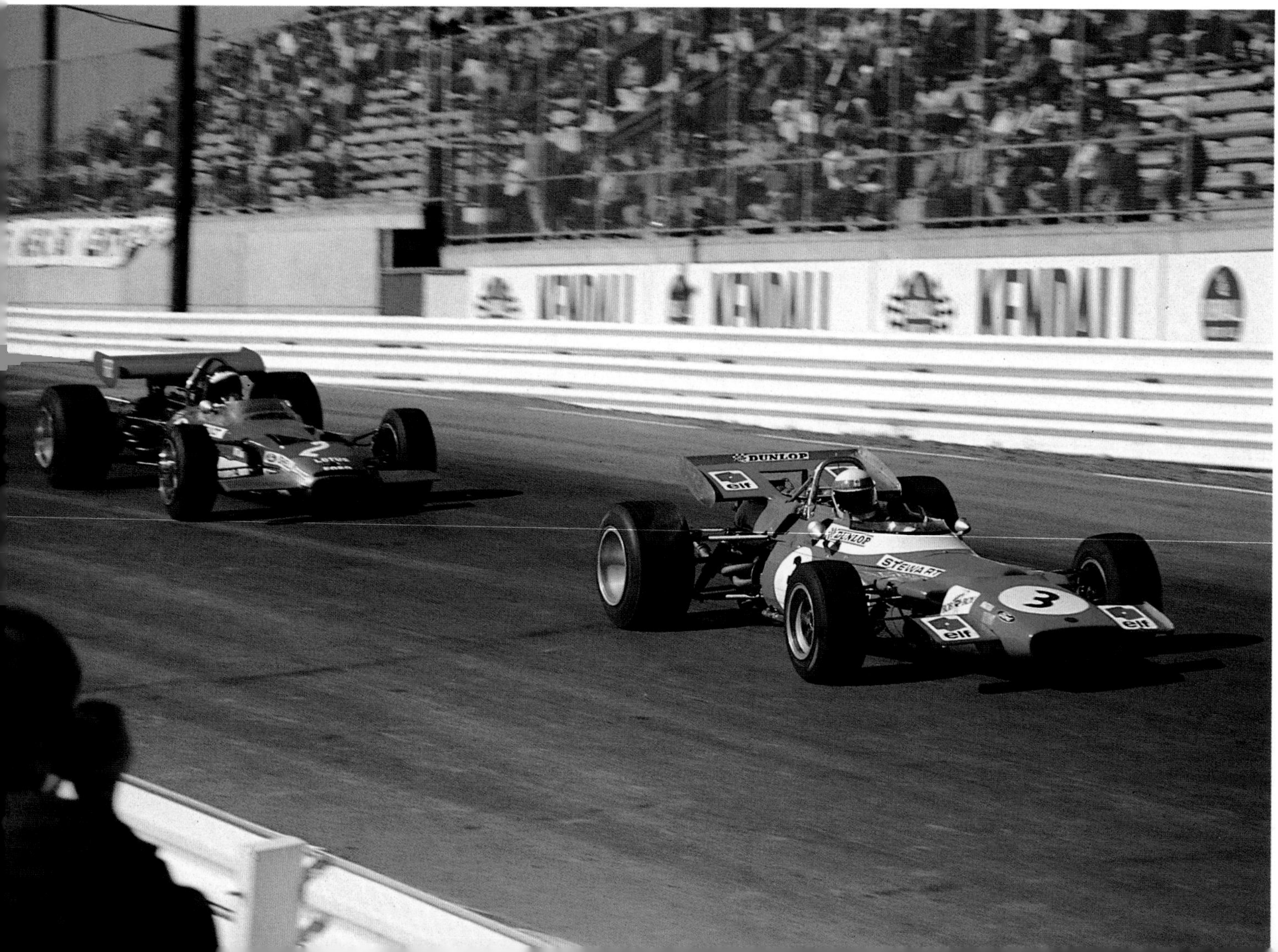

DUNLOP
elf
elf
DUNLOP

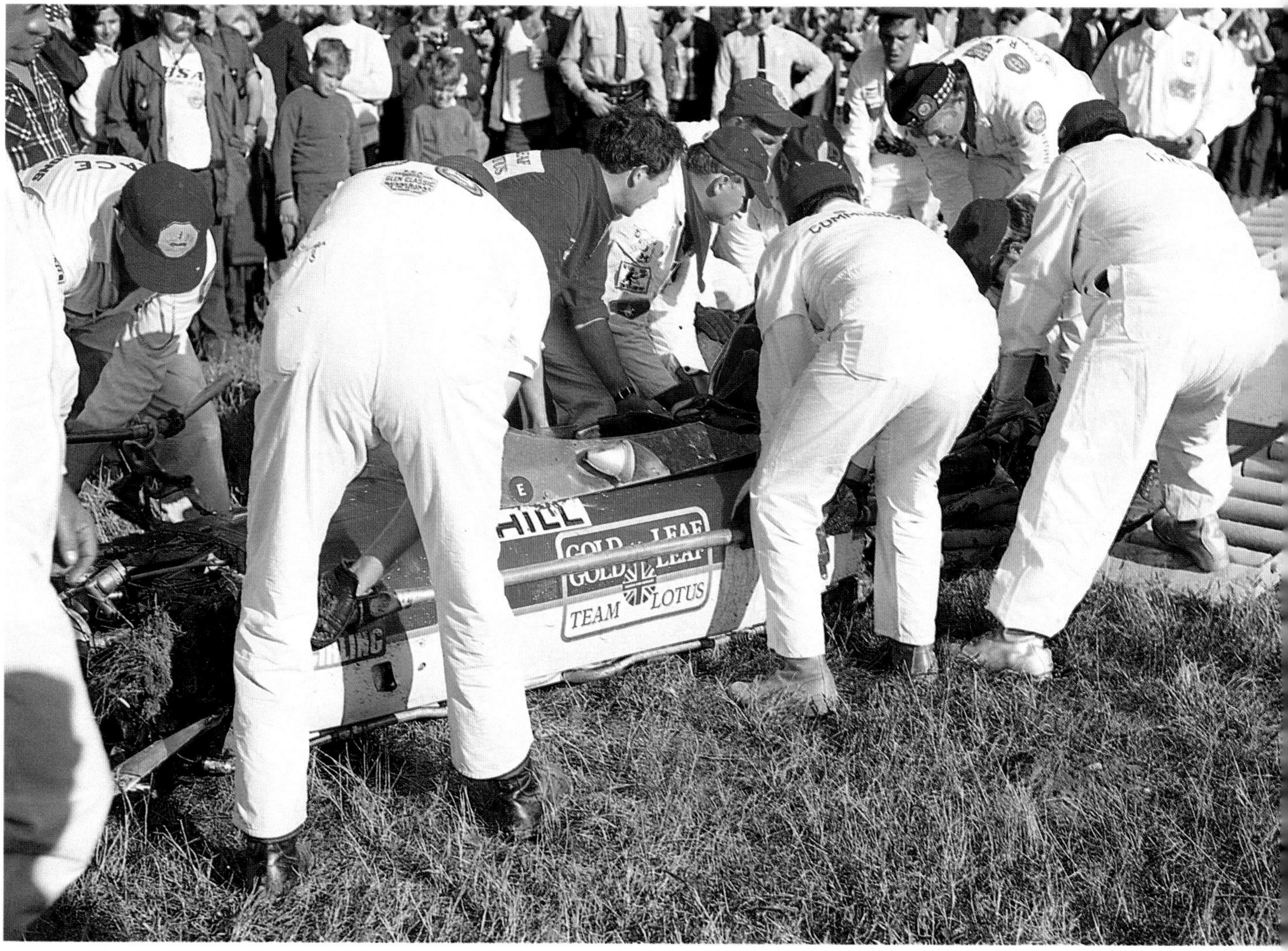

**(Top)** Graham Hill suffered severe leg injuries in the 1969 U.S. Grand Prix. He managed to push-start his Lotus after spinning off course with 18 laps remaining, but was unable to secure his safety belts. He was planning to pit to get belted up, but he cut a tire at the end of the back-straight, sending the Lotus cartwheeling and ejecting Hill from the car. The popular driver made a remarkable recovery.

**(Left)** A typical camping scene from the 1969 U.S. Grand Prix. Over the years, many fans have enjoyed camping at the scenic circuit.

**Graham Hill in the Rob Walker Racing Ford-powered Lotus.**

(**Right**) Jochen Rindt holds aloft the trophy after capturing the 1969 U.S. Grand Prix in a Lotus. He never defended his title. Rindt lost his life in practice for the Italian Grand Prix in 1970 at Monza. He scored enough points prior to the accident to become the only driver to win the World Championship posthumously. Miss Grand Prix is Dawn Ruuspakka of Newfield, N.Y., while Colin Chapman is at the far left.

(**Below**) A large crowd cheers Jochen Rindt to his 1969 Grand Prix victory.

**(Top Right)** The talented Frenchman, Francois Cevert, Jackie Stewart's Tyrell teammate, posts his solitary Grand Prix victory — the 1971 race at Watkins Glen.

**(Right)** Pedro Rodriguez finished second in the 1970 U.S. Grand Prix in a BRM. It was his best finish in six Grands Prix at The Glen. It was also his final appearance in the U.S. Grand Prix, with the Mexican losing his life the following July in an Interseries race at the Norisring in Germany.

"I remember my first race at Watkins Glen so vividly, because the first race I ever did in the United States was at Watkins Glen, driving for Ferrari in 1968 in the United States Grand Prix, and it was my second race for Ferrari, so I remember The Glen vividly for many, many reasons. That was my first impression of America.

"Two years later, I came back and drove for John Surtees, and my best result in Formula One was at The Glen, winning the only point I ever got in the World Championship.

"The Glen really brought forth to me the enthusiasm of the American public for road racing.

"To me, The Glen is the home of road racing in the United States."

DEREK BELL

**(Above)** John Surtees awaits the start of the 1970 Grand Prix. The 1964 World Champion, his final Formula One appearance was at The Glen in 1972, when he practiced but did not race due to an engine shortage on his team.

**(Top)** Englishman Derek Bell gets advice from veteran John Surtees prior to the 1970 U.S. Grand Prix. The race was Bell's fifth Formula One start, and he came home with his only career points-scoring finish, a sixth. Bell would have much better success in sports car racing, both internationally and at Watkins Glen.

**(Right)** Colorful starter Tex Hopkins flags off the 1970 U.S. Grand Prix, in front of the Red, White and Blue grandstands. The following year, the circuit would be rebuilt and the start/finish line relocated to its present location.

**(Below)** Jack Brabham's final appearance at The Glen was in the 1970 U.S. Grand Prix, in which he finished 10th in a Brabham BT-33. While Sir Jack never won at The Glen, his son Geoff would become a multi-time winner in IMSA competition.

**(Below Right)** Emerson Fittipaldi meets the media following his victory. Note Chris Economaki filing a report directly behind Fittipaldi, and Watkins Glen starter Tex Hopkins (with cigar).

**(Right)** Emerson Fittipaldi surprised the racing world by winning the 1970 U.S. Grand Prix in a Lotus in only his fourth Formula One start. Fittipaldi's victory was a great emotional lift for Team Lotus who had lost their team leader less than a month earlier when Jochen Rindt (the 1970 World Champion) lost his life practicing for the Italian Grand Prix at Monza.

**(Below)** Emerson Fittipaldi at speed in the Gold Leaf Lotus during the 1970 U.S. Grand Prix.

"For me, 1970 was not only the first time I came to Watkins Glen, but it was the first time I came to the United States. I remember there was a lot of excitement, and I was under tremendous pressure.

"For sure, Watkins Glen was the beginning of my Grand Prix career. It was a very important win, my first win, and I have great memories of Watkins Glen. I love the place, I love the people."

EMERSON FITTIPALDI

Watkins Glen was important enough that I always felt it was my home track, even though I didn't live in New York state. Obviously they had the Grand Prix there, but the Six Hour race was also pretty important. You had some foreign element, you had some chance to test yourself. It's a great, great racetrack.

SKIP BARBER

**(Left)** Known today as the head of the multi-level driving school that bears his name, Skip Barber was a top competitor in open-wheeled cars in the late Sixties and early Seventies. He ran five Formula One races in a privately-owned March, including The Glen in 1971 and 1972.

**(Center Left)** Joakim Bonnier was a very popular figure at The Glen since his victory in the 1958 Formula Libre race. He drove in 10 Formula One races at The Glen, with his best finishes sixth in 1961 and 1966. The Swede lost his life at LeMans in 1972.

**(Below Left)** Peter Revson waits by his Yardley McLaren during practice for the 1972 Grand Prix. He ran in three U.S. Grands Prix, with his best finish a fifth in 1973.

**(Below)** Jo Siffert prepares for the start of the 1970 U.S. Grand Prix. He finished ninth after qualifying his March on the back row.

**(Left)** The Watkins Glen circuit was expanded from 2.3 to 3.377 miles in 1971. The major addition was four new turns at the southeast end of the circuit, known as the "Boot" or "Anvil." The turns were designed with elevated viewing areas to enhance the spectator's experience. Fans get to see action in the Boot for the first time in the 1971 Grand Prix, won by Tyrrell's Francois Cevert.

**(Below Left)** Skip Barber leads a group of cars into the Boot in 1972. He's followed by the March of Henri Pescarolo, the March of Ronnie Peterson, Andrea De Adamich on the outside in a Surtees, Patrick Depailler in a Tyrrell, Jean-Pierre Beltoise in a BRM, Mike Beuttler in a March, and Niki Lauda, making his Glen debut in a March.

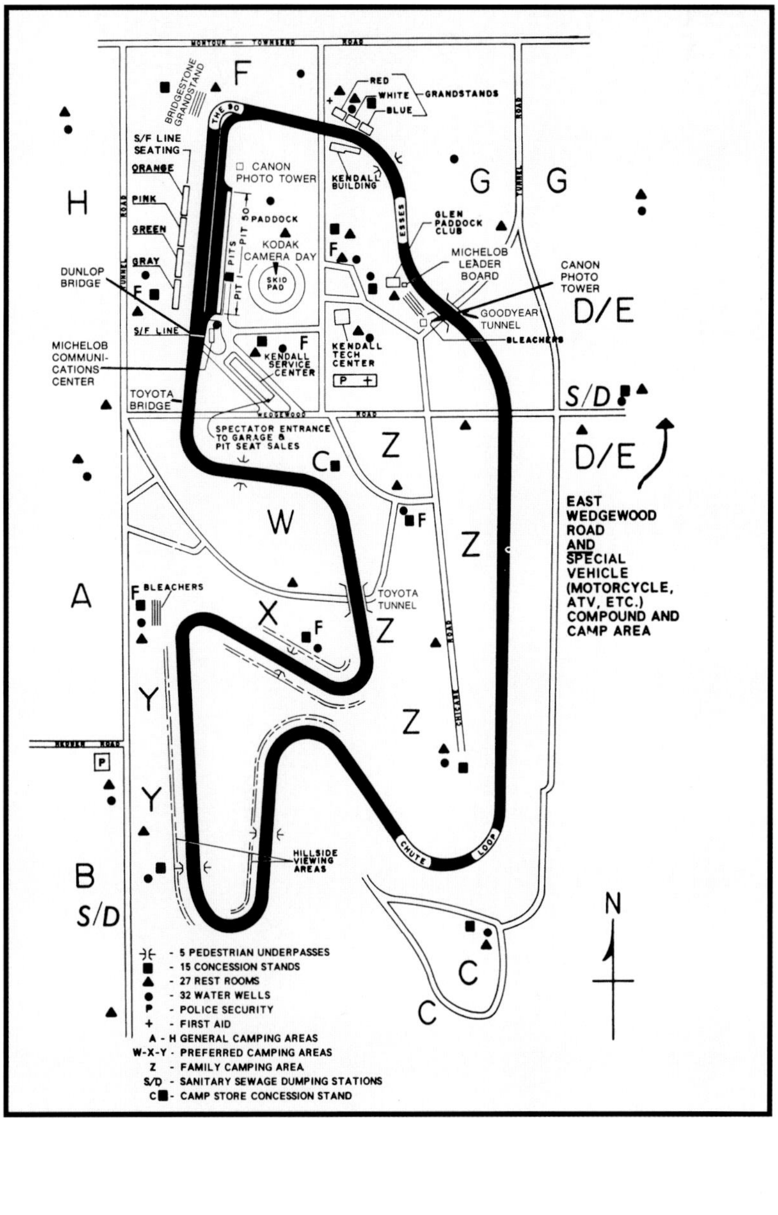


**(Top)** Jacky Ickx had his best finish of nine Watkins Glen U.S. Grands Prix with a fourth place finish in 1970, driving a Ferrari 312B.

**(Above)** 1970 action sees Reine Wisell, No. 23 Lotus, lead a group including the Surtees of Derek Bell, George Eaton in a BRM, and the No. 15 Brabham of Jack Brabham.

**(Right)** Map of the 3.377-mile circuit, used from 1971-1991.

**(Above)** Tex Hopkins waves the green flag for the 1972 U.S. Grand Prix. With pole sitter and eventual winner Jackie Stewart already out of the picture, the Yardley McLarens of Peter Revson (No. 20) and Denis Hulme (No. 19), the Brabham of Carlos Reutemann (No. 26) and the Tyrrell of Francois Cevert (No. 2) pull away.

**(Center Right)** Cars arrive at The Glen for the 1973 Grand Prix. Contrast the scene with today's huge transporters.

**(Lower Right)** Clay Regazzoni's BRM is unloaded prior to the opening of practice for the 1973 U.S. Grand Prix. All Grand Prix cars were transported to Toronto for the Grand Prix of Canada and then trucked to The Glen.

**(Above)** Jackie Stewart at speed during the 1972 U.S. Grand Prix in his Tyrrell.

**(Right)** Ken Tyrrell holds up the trophy after Jackie Stewart's second victory at The Glen.

**(Far Right)** Scotsman Jackie Stewart was greeted by bagpipes when he pulled into Victory Circle following the 1972 U.S. Grand Prix.

Jackie Stewart shows the strain of the race from Victory Circle after winning the 1972 U.S. Grand Prix.

Now fully recovered, Stewart gives a winner's kiss to his wife, Helen.

**(Above)** Francois Cevert sits in his Tyrrell prior to practice for the 1973 U.S. Grand Prix. He was killed that Saturday morning in a violent crash in the Esses.

**(Left)** Mal Currie, director of the Grand Prix Corporation, offers condolences to Jackie Stewart following the death of his friend and teammate on the eve of the 1973 Grand Prix. Stewart retired from racing that day, ending a career in which he won 27 races in 99 starts.

**(Right)** Ronnie Peterson heads to victory in a John Player Team Lotus in the 1973 Grand Prix.

**(Below)** Ronnie Peterson holds the trophy after winning the 1973 U.S. Grand Prix, his fourth victory of the season for Lotus. The Swedish star was one of the greatest and most successful Grand Prix drivers never to win the World Championship.

Ronnie Peterson, head down, concentrating hard, just staved off rookie James Hunt's pursuits throughout the 1973 U.S. Grand Prix. Hunt set fast lap in the race and went on to finish second. Here, in the early stages, out in the Boot, Peterson, in a Lotus 72, leads Reutermann's Brabham, Hunt's Hesketh March, Fitapaldi's Lotus, Hailwood's Surtees and Hulme and Revson in McLarens.

(Above) Carlos Reutemann's Brabham leads James Hunt's Hesketh during the 1974 U.S. Grand Prix. Reutemann won after a race-long duel, while Hunt's brakes faded in the closing laps and he finished third. In 1973, Hunt's rookie year, the Englishman set fast lap and finished second.

(Right) Emerson Fittipaldi only finished fourth, but that was enough to clinch his second World Championship in 1974. Both Clay Regazzoni and rookie Jody Scheckter entered the race with a shot at the title.

Carlos Reutemann of Argentina won his first of two U.S. Grands Prix in 1974, driving a Brabham.

**(Left)** A large crowd of supporters was on hand to congratulate Emerson Fittipaldi on winning the 1974 World Championship.

**(Below Left)** Emerson Fittipaldi won his first of two World Championships in this John Player Special Lotus 72D.

**(Below)** Racing on his 30th birthday, Carlos Pace finished second to Brabham teammate Carlos Reutemann at The Glen in 1974. The Brazilian lost his life in a plane crash in Brazil early in the 1977 season.

**(Bottom)** James Hunt had a stellar career at The Glen. In six Grands Prix, driving for Hesketh Racing and for Team McLaren, Hunt had five top-five finishes, captured two poles and won in 1976 and 1977.

**(Above)** Niki Lauda (left) leads the McLaren of Emerson Fittipaldi during the 1975 U.S. Grand Prix, as they prepare to lap the Copersucar Fittipaldi of Wilson Fittipaldi. The elder brother of the two-time World Champion finished 10th in his 36th and final Grand Prix.

**(Below)** Niki Lauda in his World Championship-winning Ferrari 312T.

**(Above)** A new challenge for the Grand Prix competitors in 1975 was the chicane below the Esses, designed by Jody Scheckter, who negotiates the chicane in his Tyrrell.

**(Left)** Car owner Graham Hill chats with Tony Brise prior to the 1975 Grand Prix. Both men, along with four crewmen, lost their lives the following month in a crash of a private plane carrying the Embassy Hill team, returning to England from a test in France.

My first year in Formula One I thought The Glen was a very difficult circuit. It was nice to drive. It was not easy, it was a little bit dangerous, but that's part of motor racing. It was always nice to be back at The Glen. I remember winning the golf tournament twice. It is a nice place, and I always enjoy racing there.

CLAY REGAZZONI

**(Top)** While Niki Lauda led the entire race on his way to his 1975 victory, teammate Clay Regazzoni's lapped car got between Lauda and second place runner Emerson Fittipaldi for several laps. When Regazzoni was black flagged, he dropped out of the race in anger.

**(Above)** While best known at The Glen for his consistent drives in sports cars, German Jochen Mass also competed in six U.S. Grands Prix. His best finish was a very competitive third in 1975, driving for Team McLaren.

**(Right)** Niki Lauda was a flag-to-flag winner of the 1975 U.S. Grand Prix in a Ferrari.

**(Far Right)** The total concentration required of a Formula One driver is evident in Niki Lauda's eyes as he prepares for the start of the 1976 Grand Prix.

**(Right and Below)** Clay Regazzoni raced at The Glen from 1970 through 1979. The hard-charging Swiss driver's best finish was a sixth for Ferrari in 1972.

**(Top)** Racing in the rain during the 1976 Grand Prix. Eventual winner James Hunt leads Mario Andretti and Carlos Reutemann as their rain tires kick up giant rooster tails of spray.

**(Left)** Hans Stuck's biggest moment at The Glen came when he led the opening laps of the 1977 Grand Prix in the rain. His day ended when his race-leading Martini Brabham jumped out of gear and crashed. He would have much better luck at The Glen racing sports cars.

(Left) James Hunt holds his first of two consecutive first place trophies in 1976. Both victories came driving for Team McLaren.

(Below) James Hunt cruises to victory in the 1977 U.S. Grand Prix.

The field takes the green light for the 1976 U.S. Grand Prix. Top contenders, left to right, include the No.1 Ferrari of Niki Lauda, the No.4 six wheeled Tyrell of Patrick Depailler, and the No.11 McLaren of James Hunt, the eventual winner.

Marlboro

RÖMERQUELLE
CHRONOGRAPH
HEUER

**(Right)** Brabham team owner Bernie Ecclestone chats with James Hunt prior to the 1979 U.S. Grand Prix. Today, Eccelstone is the most powerful man in Grand Prix racing, as head of the Formula One Constructors Association.

**(Below Left)** Frank Williams visited Victory Circle at The Glen in 1980, when Alan Jones won the U.S. Grand Prix. Williams first entry at Watkins Glen was in 1969, when Piers Courage brought his Brabham home third.

**(Below Right)** Scranton, Pa., native Ted Mayer relocated to England to head Team McLaren, which won the 1976 and 1977 U.S. Grands Prix.

**(Opposing Page)** Austrian Niki Lauda won the 1975 World Championship. He suffered a near-fatal crash at Nurburgring, Germany, the following year but staged a remarkable recovery. Lauda went on to win two more world titles, in 1977 for Ferrari and 1984 for McLaren.

(Top Left) One of the most unusual cars to compete at The Glen was this six-wheeled Tyrrell, which Scheckter steered to a second place finish in 1976.

(Above) Close up of "Project 34," the tiny 12-inch front wheels, which were designed to improve traction while reducing drag.

(Center Left) Scheckter joined Walter Wolf in 1977. He followed up a third place finish at The Glen with a victory in Canada.

(Below Left) Jody Scheckter made his Grand Prix debut at The Glen in 1972, finishing ninth in a Yardley McLaren.

(Below) Jody Scheckter in the cockpit of his Tyrrell in 1974.

(Opposing Page) Jody Scheckter began and finished his Formula One career at Watkins Glen, ending up with an 11th for Ferrari in 1980. In between, he won 10 races and the 1979 World Championship.

Mario Andretti returned to The Glen in 1978 as a conquering hero, having clinched the World Championship at the prior race at Monza. Andretti joined Phil Hill (1961) as the only Americans to win the World Championship.

Mario Andretti won six races and the 1978 World Championship, with five of the victories coming in this revolutionary "ground effects" Lotus 79.

The wing of Andretti's Lotus tells of his championship season.

The crowd came out en masse to welcome Mario.

Part of the huge crowd for the 1978 U.S. Grand Prix, won by Carlos Reutemann over Alan Jones.

Mario Andretti won the pole, but raceday was a huge disappointment. He crashed his Lotus in warmups, and the engine expired on the backup car during the race, resulting in a DNF.

"It was very disappointing, because I think I could have won that year hands down, as far as the car was concerned.

"But we had a brake problem, and The Glen doesn't forgive.

MARIO ANDRETTI

**(Right)** Young Canadian Gilles Villeneuve won the 1979 U.S. Grand Prix. At right is Ferrari engineer Antonio Tomaini.

**(Below)** Gilles Villeneuve leaves the pits during practice in his Ferrari 312T5.

**(Opposing Page)** Gilles Villeneuve is a study in intensity prior to the 1979 Grand Prix. Racing was robbed of one of its brightest stars when he lost his life in an accident during practice for the 1982 Belgian Grand Prix at Zolder. His son, Jacques, won the 1997 World Championships.

Marlboro
Labatt

With Lake Seneca in the background, the field roars away for the start of the 1980 U.S. Grand Prix. Who knew that this would be the final appearance of the Formula One series at The Glen?

(**Left**) Gilles Villeneuve takes the checkered flag, winning the 1979 Grand Prix in a Scuderia Ferrari 312T4. The retired Gitanes Ligier of Jacques Lafitte is parked just before the finish line.

(**Center**) Alan Jones — the winner of the last U.S. Grand Prix at Watkins Glen.

(**Below**) Alan Jones drives to victory in the 1980 U.S. Grand Prix, driving a Williams FW07.

# Professional Sports Car Racing

## A Variety of New Traditions

While Watkins Glen was America's address on the international Grand Prix tour from 1961 through 1980, the circuit also hosted a wide variety of other events. Professional sports car racing came into its own in the early Sixties, and The Glen hosted the USRRC, Trans-Am, Can-Am, Formula 5000, and the World Endurance Championship.

In addition, The Glen held many other races, including CART Indy cars, NASCAR Grand National, snowmobiles, and NASCAR-style late models and modifieds.

"When you think about it, I drove many different types of cars at Watkins Glen — Formula 5000, Formula One, sports cars, Can-Am cars, stock cars with the IROC, and Indy cars," said Mario Andretti, the 1978 World Champion. "The Glen is probably the only track where I drove five or six disciplines of cars. With so many different cars, and so many variety of cars, you're going to have your ups and downs, the peaks and valleys. I certainly experienced that at Watkins Glen."

The Glen's annual Sports Car Grand Prix evolved into the United States Road Racing Championships — which in turn led to the Can-Am Championship. The Glen Classic became The Glen 500, which paved the way for the Trans-Am.

A field of thundering unlimited horsepower Can-Am cars roars past the pits after taking the green flag. Among the top drivers in the 1972 event are (left to right) Jackie Oliver in the No. 101 Shadow, Francois Cevert in the No. 22 McLaren, pole winner Peter Revson in the No. 4 McLaren, George Follmer in the L&M Porsche 917, and Denis Hulme in the No. 5 McLaren. Hulme went on to score his second Watkins Glen Can-Am victory, the fourth straight at The Glen for Team McLaren.

"I was fortunate to race in the most intense period of Trans-Am competition, in which Parnelli Jones, Peter Revson, George Follmer and Mark Donohue were racing — an incredible collection of fast, excellent drivers," recalled Brock Yates, a columnist for Car and Driver who wrote the book "Sunday Driver" based on his experiences in The Glen's 1971 Trans-Am event. "I remember going down the front straight, being bracketed by Follmer and Donohue, who passed me as if I was running in some other class of car.

"Racing at The Glen was like playing baseball in Yankee Stadium," Yates added.

The Glen's summer sports car events included plenty of international flavor, especially the annual Six Hours, a stop on the World Endurance Championship series schedule. The Six Hours brought over top European teams and drivers, racing against America's top sports car teams.

"I just love The Glen — because it was the first track I had been to in America," said Derek Bell. "Because I had my only World Championship point there. Because I won several sports car races — and raced Formula 5000 there. I had lots of reasons to race there. And I loved The Glen — it was like my home circuit in North America. To me, The Glen is the home of road racing in the United States."

The Mid-Seventies brought the Formula 5000 series, for powerful open-wheeled cars. It attracted drivers from both sports car and Indy car racing, and the result was excellent, popular competition.

"Watkins Glen is a tremendous place, with a lot of history and beautiful scenery," said Brian Redman, who dominated Formula 5000 racing at The Glen in addition to racing in Formula One, the World Endurance Championship, Can-Am and Camel GTP.

"I was fortunate to run the fastest lap ever back in 1975, in a Formula 5000 car," Redman added. "I didn't get much publicity from that, breaking Mark Donohue's record in a Can-Am car, but I was very happy with that — it was faster than the Formula One record and it stood for quite a time. I've had very good races at The Glen in Formula 5000 — and a few very big frights. Formula 5000 was an

**(Above)** Ford driver Peter Revson leads the Camaro of eventual winner Mark Donohue during The Glen's 1969 Trans-Am.

extremely tough series, because it brought together top drivers from all facets of racing."

In the late Seventies, The Glen hosted the second generation Can-Am, plus the CART Indy car series, drawing in a new group of star drivers.

"Watkins Glen is a great track," said Danny Sullivan, who finished second in The Glen's 1980 Can-Am. "It's a fabulous place. When you go to a place with that much tradition, that much history, I've always found there is a reason there's that much history, and that means they are our favorite tracks, and Watkins Glen rates right up there."

While professional sports car racing dominated The Glen's summer schedule, the tradition of SCCA amateur competion continued. Annually, The Glen Nationals and other club events attracted the country's top sports car drivers, with regular winners including Bob Sharp, Bob Tullius, Oscar Koveleski, Bertil Roos and Paul Newman.

"The Glen had more history than any race track I'd ever run," recalled Sharp. "In college, we'd borrow a spare tent from a friend who had a tent renting business, and go to the races. I've got fond memories. At The Glen, you could watch people race you only read about in the magazines.

"The Glen is a very special place," continued the Connecticut businessman. "It has something beyond what other tracks offer — a nostalgia — something some people take for granted. It's very special to win at The Glen. You just can't get away from its history."

**(Above)** Tex Hopkins is in fine form, waving off the field for the 1961 Grand Prix. On the pole is Roger Penske in a Cooper Monaco, flanked by the Briggs Cunningham-owned Maserati of Walt Hansgen. Car No. 1 is the Scarab of Harry Heuer.

**(Right)** In one of the closest finishes in Glen racing history, Dr. M.R.J. Wyllie's Lola edges the Lola of Francis Bradley in the 1961 Queen Catharine Cup.

(**Above**) The field is ready for start of the 1962 Seneca Cup.

(**Center Left**) George Constantine passed Walt Hansgen with only two laps remaining and went on to win the 1961 Sports Car Grand Prix in a Ferrari.

(**Center Right**) Versatile Bob Bucher came out of retirement and added to his Glen trophy collection by winning the 1961 Glen Classic in a Porsche Spyder RSK.

(**Lower Right**) Walt Hansgen wears the laurel wreath as he accepts congratulations from starter Tex Hopkins after winning the 1962 Seneca Cup in a Cooper Formula Jr.

**(Right)** The Glen Classic gave way to The Glen 500 in 1964. Hal Keck (left) and Oscar Koveleski celebrate their victory in the 1965 Glen 500, driving a Cobra in the 500-mile race.

**(Lower Left)** Connecticut driver Bob Sharp is a winner in one of his first Watkins Glen appearances, winning the Schuyler Carrera race during the 1965 Glen 500 weekend, driving a Datsun Special 310.

**(Lower Right)** Two frequent Watkins Glen winners, Ed Lowther and Dr. M.R.J. Wyllie, combined to win the 1967 Glen 500 in a Cobra. It was Wyllie's final victory at The Glen, although Lowther would still be racing — and winning — in the early Eighties. In 1968, The Glen 500 was replaced by the SCCA Trans-Am Championship.

The United States Road Racing Championships debuted at The Glen in 1963. Above, Ford Cobra driver Ken Miles (No. 98) leads Ken Brown's Cobra and Mike Gammino's Ferrari at the chicane at the end of the back straight. Bob Johnson won the Manufacturer's Championship event in a Cobra. Despite the 100-degree temperatures, Miles refueled his car following the race and drove to a third place finish behind the Porsches of Bob Holbert and Herb Swan in the USRRC Driver's Championship event.

**(Left)** Glen's 1966 USRRC race, won by Lola driver John "Buck" Fulp in an upset. On the pole is Jerry Grant's Lola T-70. Mark Donohue, driving Lola-Chevy No. 6, escaped with minor burns from a fiery accident in the Esses early in the race.

**(Center Left)** Sam Posey finished second in the 1967 USRRC race in a McLaren. Mark Donohue won the race to clinch the series' championship, with Skip Barber placing third.

**(Center Right)** Peter Revson was held up at the start of the 1967 USRRC race by a stalled car, but ran the fastest lap of the race in his McLaren trying to catch up. A blown engine ended his day.

**(Lower Left)** Buck Fulp of Anderson, S.C. won the 1966 USRRC in this Lola T-70, following Mark Donohue's crash in the Esses.

**(Lower Right)** While this crash destroyed Bob Bondurant's McLaren and ended his racing days, it marked the beginning of a very successful career as a racing driving instructor.

SIMONIZ
SIMONIZ
SUNOCO

**(Above)** A new era begins with the start of the inaugural Six Hours for the FIA World Manufacturer's Championship in 1968. Jo Siffert won the pole in a Porsche 908.

**(Left)** Lucien Bianchi joins Jackie Ickx in the winning Ford GT40 at The Glen's first Six Hour race.

**(Opposing Page)** The grid is set for the start of The Glen's final USRRC race in 1968. Sam Posey led the opening 21 laps in his Caldwell (No. 1), but lost oil pressure and retired. Mark Donohue (No. 6, barely visible at left) won the race by two laps over Chuck Parsons' Lola (No. 10). In 1969, the USRRC was replaced by the Can-Am.

Vic Elford leads the field in the 1970 Six Hours in the Porsche 917 he co-drove with Denis Hulme. Second is eventual winner Pedro Rodriquez in another Porsche 917, followed by Georg Loos in a Ferrari 512S. Elford eventually finished fourth.

KENDALL
KENDALL
AUDI

**(Above)** The start of the 1970 Six Hours

**(Left)** A driver change on the Jo Siffert/Brian Redman Gulf Porsche 917 during the 1970 Six Hours. They went on to finish second behind teammates Pedro Rodriguez and Leo Kinnunen.

**(Right)**
Pedro Rodriquez — winner of the 1970 Six Hours.

**(Far Right)**
John Wyer times in the Gulf Porsche pits during the 1970 Six Hours. His team won the Six Hours in 1968, 1969 and 1970.

**(Below)**
Len Kinnunen hitches a ride into Victory Circle with co-driver Pedro Rodriguez after winning the 1970 Six Hours. Sitting on the left side of the car is crew chief Ermanno Cuoghi.

**(Top)** Richard Attwood, driving a Porsche 917, leads the Alfa Romeo 33/3 of Andrea DeAdamich early in the 1971 Six Hours. With the new "Boot" under construction, drivers ran the new 2.428 mile short course. DeAdamich and Ronnie Peterson went on to win, giving Alfa Romeo its first major victory at The Glen since 1948.

**(Center)** Jacky Ickx leads the field to the start of the 1972 Six Hours. Ickx teamed with Mario Andretti to win in a Ferrari 312P. Also up front are second place finisher Ronnie Peterson in the No. 86 Ferrari 312P, Arturo Merzario in the No. 87 Ferrari 312P, and third place finisher Derek Bell in the No.10 Gulf Mirage.

**(Left)** Jacky Ickx steers the Ferrari 312P he shared with Mario Andretti to victory circle after their 1972 Six Hours victory.

**(Opposing Page)** Mario Andretti (left) and Jacky Ickx celebrate after winning the 1972 Six Hours. Joining in the victory circle action are Andretti's sons, Michael (left-center) and Jeff.

WATKINS GLEN GRAND PRIX
DAYTONA
BEACH

(Left) Henri Pescarolo (left) and Gerald Larrouse celebrate their victory in the 1973 Six Hours. French manufacturer Matro won back-to-back victories in the Six Hours, with Jeane-Pierre Jarier teaming with Jean-Pierre Beltoise to win in 1974.

(Center) Henri Pescarolo and Gerald Larrouse won the 1973 Six Hours in this Matra.

(Below) Jean-Pierre Jarier and Jean-Pierre Beltoise shared the winning Matra-Simca 670C in the 1974 Six Hours.

"It was a very good time with Matra. I had a very good souvenir from Watkins Glen. It's a track I like very much, and there was big competition all the time, and it was a very big win for me."

HENRI PESCAROLO

**(Top)** Peter Gregg (left) and protege Hurley Haywood win the Trans-Am portion of the 1974 Six Hours, during the "Five Star" Weekend.

**(Left)** The Brumos Porsche Carrera of Peter Gregg and Hurley Haywood, shown in turn nine, finished third overall in the 1974 Six Hours, scoring double points for winning the Trans-Am class during the event. This was one of Haywood's nine victories at The Glen, making him the circuit's most successful professional driver.

**(Right)**
Jody Scheckter, in the Elf Renault Alpine, leads the field at the start of the 1975 Six Hours. Just behind Scheckter is Mario Andretti in the Campari Alfa Romeo 33TT12, which finished second, and the Alfa Romeo 33TT12 of eventual winners Derek Bell and Henri Pescarolo.

**(Center Left)** Henri Pescarolo and Derek Bell chat prior to the 1975 Six Hours.

**(Center Right)** Henri Pescarolo and Derek Bell co-drove this Alfa Romeo 33TT12 to win the 1975 Six Hours.

**(Below Left)** It's a driver change for Renault Alpine teammates Gerald Larrouse and Jean-Pierre Jarier during the 1975 Six Hours. They finished third.

**(Below Right)** Team Alfa Prepares for the 1975 Six Hours.

**(Top Left)** Benny Parsons, the 1973 NASCAR Winston Cup champion and 1975 Daytona 500 winner, co-drove a BMW with Hans Stuck during the 1977 Six Hours.

**(Top Right)** Jochen Mass and Jacky Ickx overcame turbocharger trouble to win the 1977 Six Hours.

**(Center Left)** Jochen Mass (left) shares a quick word with Jacky Ickx during a driver change in the 1977 Six Hours.

**(Lower Left)** Brian Redman and Indy car pioneer Janet Guthrie co-drove to eighth place in a Porsche 935T in the 1978 Six Hours.

**(Below Right)** The Mass/Ickx Martini Porsche 935T led all but 53 laps during the 1977 Six Hours.

**(Bottom Right)** Bob Tullius and Brian Feurstenau co-drove the Group 44 Jaguar SJ-S to the Trans-Am I class victory in the 1978 Six Hours.

**Fuels spills during Hal Shaw Racing's pit stop...**

**...It suddenly ignites...**

**...And the Porsche bursts into flames. Four crewmen were treated for burns resulting from this incident.**

"I love going to Watkins Glen. It's a real classic race track, probably one of the most demanding racetracks in North America. Peter Gregg had decided for my first race we're going to run a world championship race at Watkins Glen. I arrived there, I had just turned 21, and none of the officials had heard of me, but they had to give me a license, and we went on and won that race. That was quite an experience."

HURLEY HAYWOOD

**(Top)** Two of endurance racing's all-time greats, Brian Redman (left) and Hurley Haywood, chat during a break in the action during the 1978 Six Hours. Both drivers enjoyed success at The Glen in a variety of cars and races.

**(Center)** The Whittington Brothers Porsche 935T en route to victory in the 1979 Six Hours.

**(Below)** Brothers Don (left) and Bill Whittington flank Klaus Ludwig after winning the 1979 Six Hours in a Porsche 935T.

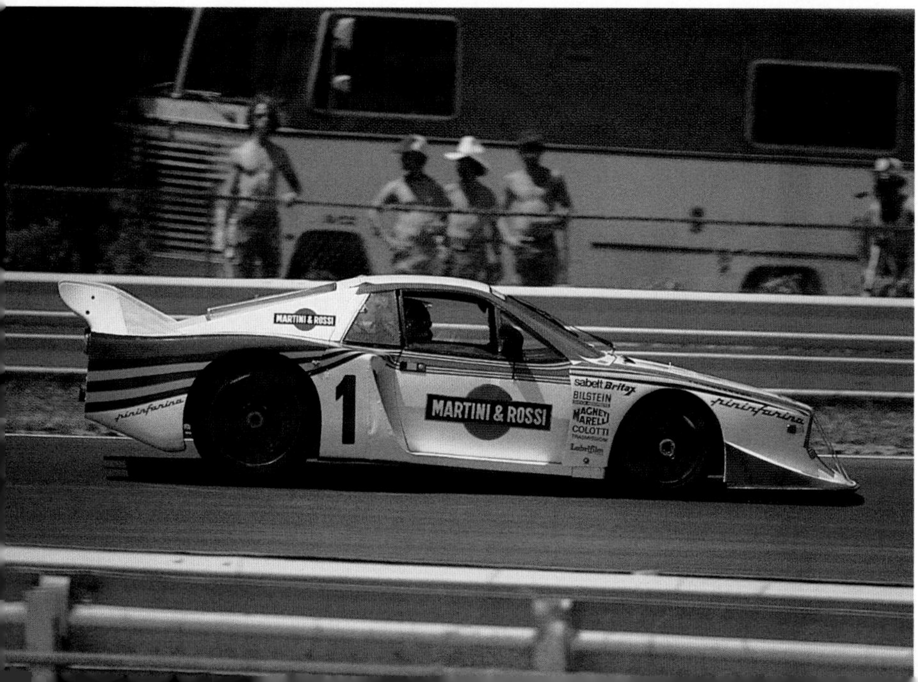


**(Left)** The Lancia Corse Italia team dominated the final two runnings of the original Six Hours in 1980 and 1981.

**(Lower Left)** Riccardo Patrese returned to win the 1981 Six Hours, this time joined by Michele Alboreto in a Lancia Monte Carlo.

**(Below Right)** The drivers of the eventual second place Porsche meet prior to the 1979 Six Hours. Left to right are Rolf Stommelen, Dick Barbour and Paul Newman. While better known as an actor, Newman returned to The Glen the following month and posted a pair of overall victories in the SCCA Bonus Nationals, driving Bob Sharp Datsuns.

**(Bottom Right)** Riccardo Patrese and Hans Heyer visit Victory Circle following the 1980 Six Hours.

**(Top)** The start of the 1971 Trans-Am has George Follmer's Ford Mustang and Mark Donohue's AMC Javelin on the front row.

**(Center)** Jerry Titus takes the checkered flag to win The Glen's inaugural Trans-Am race in 1968, driving a Carroll Shelby Ford Mustang. When he wasn't racing, Titus was editor of Sports Car Graphic magazine.

**(Below)** Parnelli Jones (15) and Mark Donohue (6) staged memorable Trans-Am battles from 1969 to 1971. This is The Glen in '71, the first year of new configuration. Pit entrance is just visible at bottom of photo.

(**Top**) Vic Elford made the right choices for tires in changing weather conditions, and came up with an impressive victory in the 1970 Trans-Am, winning in Jim Hall's Chaparral Camaro, pictured top right.

(**Right**) Master mechanic Smokey Yunick ran "the best damn garage in town," and a pretty good race team, the A.J. Foyt Chevrolet-sponsored Camaro for Indy car driver Swede Savage.

(**Bottom**) The cars are set on the starting grid for the 1972 Trans-Am.

**(Top Left)** Indy car star Parnelli Jones was a top competitor in the Trans-Am championship. **(Lower Left)** Once a top sports car driver, Roger Penske was a respected car owner in the Trans-Am and other series. **(Top Right)** Versatile Peter Revson also was a frequent competitor in the Trans-Am. **(Lower Right)** The winner of the 1964 and 1965 USRRC races at The Glen, Jim Hall returned to the Trans-Am as owner of Team Chaparral.

**(Right)** Bruce McLaren leads Denis Hulme as the distinctive orange McLarens dominate the 1969 Glen Can-Am.

**(Below)** Bruce McLaren holds the trophies after winning The Glen's 1969 Can-Am. Note the legendary Stirling Moss, representing series sponsor Johnson Wax, at the right, and racing historian Bill Green at the far left.

**(Opposing Page)** Denis Hulme wins his second Can-Am race at The Glen in 1972. The strong showing of the McLaren team and its pair of Formula One aces led the Can-Am at its heyday to be nicknamed, "The Bruce and Denny Show."

Gulf
N.Y.
GOODYEAR

**(Above)** Mark Donohue began racing — and winning — in sports cars and the USRRC. With the backing of car owner Roger Penske and sponsor Sunoco, he took his winning ways to both the Trans-Am and Can-Am Series and was always the man to beat. Away from the track the personable driver earned his nickname ... 'Captain Nice'.

**(Right)** Another race, another win — Mark Donohue wins the 1969 Trans-Am in Roger Penske's Camaro.

"I know that Watkins Glen was one of my favorite tracks. I remember running the Formula One car the first time, and also when Mark Donohue had the very bad accident in the USRRC races. Watkins Glen is the history of road racing in the Northern Tier of New York state. It brings back a lot of memories of when I first got in racing."

ROGER PENSKE

**(Above)** Roger Penske (left) and Donohue celebrate the 1967 USRRC victory.

**(Below)** At his peak: Mark Donohue winning the 1973 Can-Am in the dominating Sunoco Porsche 917/30.

**The 40-car field goes down the back straight on the warmup lap for the 1970 Can-Am. Up front are the McLarens of Denis Hulme (No. 5) and Dan Gurney (No. 48); Jackie Stewart in the Chaparral (No. 66) and Peter Revson in a Lola (No. 26); and Mario Andretti in a Ferrari (No. 92).**

**(Right)** Jackie Stewart became the first consistent challenger to McLaren supremacy in the 1971 Can-Am. Aluminum Chevy engines had grown to 494 cubic engines, but would be made obsolete by turbo Porsche 917 just a year later.

**(Lower Right)** When Mark Donohue was injured testing at Road Atlanta in 1972, George Follmer filled in with five victories in Roger Penske's L&M Porsche 917/10K. At The Glen, a pit stop to fix the turbocharger resulted in a fifth place finish.

**(Top Center)** Dan Gurney leads Jackie Stewart and Peter Revson during the 1970 Can-Am.

**(Left)** Jackie Stewart was fast in the controversial "sucker" Chaparral 2J.

**(Lower Left)** The start of the second heat of the 1973 Can-Am has the Sunoco Porsche 917 of eventual winner Mark Donohue flanked by Jody Scheckter and David Hobbs.

**(Lower Center)** Peter Revson, in the L&M Lola T-220, moves low to pass the Ferrari of Jim Adams.

**(Above)** The McLarens of Denis Hulme (No.5) and Dan Gurney lead the field to the start of the 1970 Can-Am.

**(Left)** The Can-Am events always packed the house at The Glen. Gijs Van Lennep, in a Porsche 917, leads the McLaren M8D of Dan Gurney and the Lola T-220 of Peter Revson during the 1970 race.

**(Right)** George Follmer is interviewed in Victory Circle by Chris Economaki, after winning the "Shadow Challenge" during the 1974 U.S. Grand Prix weekend.

**(Below)** George Follmer drives to victory over teammates Jackie Oliver and J.P. Jarier in the Shadow Challenge, matching the cars that dominated the 1974 Can-Am in an exhibition race.

**(Inset)** Jackie Oliver went out a winner with the Can-Am at The Glen.

**(Top Left)** Jody Scheckter, the rookie sensation of the 1973 Formula 5000, totalled his Trojan Chevrolet in Friday morning practice …

**(Top Right)** … Scheckter then borrowed a Lola T-330 and coasted to victory over Brian Redman in the unfamiliar car.

**(Second Row Left)** Mario Andretti came out on top in The Glen's 1974 Formula 5000 race. Vic Franzese presents the champagne in victory circle.

**(Second Row Right)** Brian Redman won his heat and the feature in The Glen's 1975 Formula 5000 race.

**(Left)** Brian Redman definitely had all his mules pulling in the same direction in the Formula 5000 series.

**(Below Left)** Alan Jones drove to victory in his first Watkins Glen appearance, the 1976 Formula 5000 race. It was also the final Formula 5000 race at The Glen with the series replaced by the "second generation" Can-Am in 1977.

**(Top Left)** Keke Rosberg was The Glen's 1979 Can-Am winner in a Spyder NF-11.

**(Center Left)** Al Holbert drove the Holbert CRC-2 to victory in The Glen's final race for the second-generation Can-Am.

**(Below Left)** The second-generation Can-Am — basically, Formula 5000 cars with new bodywork — debuted at The Glen in 1977. Patrick Tambay drove to victory, replacing the injured Brian Redman in the Jim Hall/Carl Haas Chaparral Lola T-333CS.

**(Below Right)** The Glen's 1979 Can-Am winner, Keke Rosberg, went on to become the 1982 World Champion.

**(Bottom Right)** Geoff Brabham is greeted by brother Gary Brabham after winning The Glen's 1979 Super Vee race in a Ralt. Geoff, son of three-time World Champion Sir Jack Brabham, would return to The Glen as a dominant driver for the Nissan IMSA Camel GTP team.

"We pulled it in victory circle and we went through all the ceremonies (after winning the Cart race in 1981). When we went to back the car out of Victory Circle, the rear end locked up. All the ring and pinion bolts had backed out. So another lap and we wouldn't have finished the race. We were very fortunate."

RICK MEARS

**(Above)** Bobby Unser celebrates his first of two CART Indy Car victories at The Glen in 1979 in a Penske PC-7.

**(Top Left)** The Championship Auto Racing Teams' Indy car series paid three visits to The Glen, from 1979 through 1981. Bobby Unser won the first two races, on The Glen's 2.428-mile short course. He's shown winning the 1980 race in a Penske PC-9, driving for Roger Penske.

**(Center Left)** Unser's Penske Racing teammate, Rick Mears, won the 1981 CART race on The Glen's long course in a Penske PC-9B. That was the final race for the Grand Prix Corporation. It would be followed by two years of non-spectator events, although SCCA club racing continued at the bankrupt track.

**(Bottom Left)** Victory Circle celebrations following the Watkins Glen 200 CART race. Left to right are runnerup Johnny Rutherford, winner Rick Mears, and third place finisher Bill Alsup.

"Watkins Glen was one of my better tracks. It was one of the tracks I liked an awful lot. It was, for sure, one of my favorites. When I went there with an Indy Car, I always went fast. My races with the Indy Cars were really exciting, it was pretty easy racing — primarily because I liked the track so much."

BOBBY UNSER

# The Glen is Back!

## The Renaissance Years

The accumulated debt from rebuilding The Glen circuit took its toll in the late Seventies. The final U.S. Grand Prix at the Finger Lakes circuit was held in 1980. The Glen hosted two weekends of racing in 1981, but the Grand Prix Corporation shuttered the gates for spectator racing following a CART Indy car event on a cold, rainy October weekend.

The Glen Region of the SCCA kept alive the tradition of sports car racing with non-spectator club events, all the while searching for a potential buyer to save the circuit. Little did they know that the buyer would find them!

Jim Riesbeck, a senior executive for Corning Incorporated, marveled at the economic impact the races had on central Florida while attending the 1983 Daytona 500 as a spectator. His imagination kicked into high gear when he heard there was a vacant race track only 20 miles from Corning; and an economic impact study which proved the significant impact of the circuit on business in the region added fuel to the fire.

Corning Enterprises, a subsidiary of Corning Inc., purchased the circuit in mid-1983 and formed a partnership with International Speedway Corporation — owners of the race tracks at Daytona Beach, Talladega, Ala., and Darlington, S.C. — to manage the facility. Watkins Glen International was born!

Professional racing returned in 1984 with the first Camel Continental, a split-format IMSA Camel GT six-hour race won by the Porsche 962 of Al Holbert, Derek Bell and Jim Adams.

For 10 years, IMSA thrilled Glen fans with the exotic Camel GTP Prototypes. Above, the field is off in the 1985 New York 500. Left to right are the eventual winning Lowenbrau Porsche 962 of Al Holbert and Derek Bell; the pole-winning Coca-Cola Porsche 962 of Hans Stuck and Bob Akin, and the second place finishing BFGoodrich Porsche 962 of Jochen Mass and Jim Busby.

"It was very impressive to come back, because someone had made it a beautiful circuit," recalled Bell, a veteran of Formula One and Six Hour races at The Glen. "All the guard rails were painted, it had been manicured, it was ready to go racing again. It was a great contrast to how it had been in previous years, which was tragic, because it was such a fabulous circuit, a real European circuit."

IMSA Camel GT and SCCA Trans-Am anchored the schedule for the reborn Glen. While the addition in 1986 of the NASCAR Winston Cup Bud at The Glen completed The Glen's comeback, sports car racing continued to play a major role at The Glen.

Over the years, The Glen has attracted the fast and the famous to enjoy the festivities of speed. At the height of its popularity, marques from around the world, piloted by the finest sports car drivers, fought for Camel Continental bragging rights. Jaguars, Nissans, Toyotas and Porsches were the combatants of fierce on-track battles that filled the stands with enthusiastic fans.

The Camel Continental was a major event on The Glen's schedule through the end of the Camel GTP days. When IMSA moved to a new concept, the World Sports Car, The Glen went back to a popular format — the Six Hours — to showcase the open-cockpit prototypes.

The rebirth of the famous Six Hours also saw the renewal of the traditional sports car rivalry between Ferrari and Ford. One of the most epic struggles took place during the 1996 First Union Six Hours of The Glen

*continued on page 168*

**(Top)** Watkins Glen International dedicated a road in honor of Ralph Seagraves, retiring Director of Special Events for R.J. Reynolds Tobacco Company and a prime mover in the return of racing to The Glen. Left to right are Ed Horrigan, President and Chief Operating Officer of RJR; Seagraves; Conrad Stemski, first Chairman of the Board of Watkins Glen International; and T. Wayne Robertson, the new Director of Special Events Operations for RJR.

**(Above)** The Glen's gala reopening race, the 1984 Camel Continental, was marked by a thrilling back-and-forth battle between the Lowenbrau Porsche 962 of Derek Bell and the Blue Thunder March of Bill Whittington. The March succumbed to mechanical problems and Bell went on to win.

**(Right)** The Lowenbrau Special Porsche 962 of Al Holbert and Derek Bell won four of five IMSA Camel GT races at The Glen from 1984 through 1986.

The 1985 New York 500 was probably the most important race of my career. I think about the self confidence I had as a driver, but I hadn't demonstrated it yet, in my opinion, on the race track and in the race results. By winning at Watkins Glen, I think it sort of set the record straight in a lot of people's minds and perceptions about who Lyn St. James is as a race car driver.

LYN ST. JAMES

**(Top Left)** Lyn St. James made IMSA history by becoming the first woman to score a solo victory. She captured GTO honors in the 1985 New York 500, driving a Jack Roush Ford Mustang.

**(Center Left)** Bill Elliott took time from his "Awesome" 1985 NASCAR Winston Cup season to drive a Jack Roush Ford Mustang with Lyn St. James in the Camel Continental GTO race. He recovered from a pair of cut tires to finish fourth, breaking the track record twice in the process. At left is Ford's Michael Kranefuss with former Watkins Glen Press Director Bob Kelly at right.

**(Below Left)** Dennis Aase (center) is splashed with a Steuben bowl full of champagne following his victory in the 1988 Kodak Copier 500 IMSA Camel GTO race by Chris Cord, his co-driver with Dan Gurney's Toyata Celica team.

**(Below)** Owner-driver Rob Dyson (right) gets a few pointers from former Formula One star John Watson prior to the 1986 Camel Continental. Watson teamed with David Hobbs to finish sixth in a BMW GTP.

*continued from page 166*

with Ferrari driver "Mad" Max Papis posting a come-from-behind victory over Butch Leitzinger and Wayne Taylor. In 1997, it would be Leitzinger and Ford on the podium.

Poor attendance doomed the Trans-Am in 1985, but that resilient series returned in 1990 as a popular companion event to the Bud at The Glen.

Vintage car racing came into its own with a 1989 Ford GT40 Reunion, the largest gathering ever of that famed marquee up to that time. In following years, the Sportscar Vintage Racing Association weekend grew to become a major component of the WGI schedule.

"I think the improvements that have been done over the years have made it a lot better racetrack," said Elliott Forbes-Robinson, who has enjoyed success at The Glen for 20 years in a variety of sports cars. "It's funny how it's kept its uniqueness at the same time. The track has always been one of my favorites."

**(Top)** The Lowenbrau Special Porsche 962 takes the checkered flag for winning the 1985 Camel Continental.

**(Center)** A veteran of Formula One and World Endurance Championship racing at The Glen, popular Englishman Derek Bell returned to dominate IMSA competition at the reopened circuit.

**(Left)** The meticulous Al Holbert jots down a few notes during a practice session. The protege of Mark Donohue went on to become the leading winner in IMSA history.

"Al was an amazing organizer. He had the dealership, he had his racing team, he ran the competition side of Porsche North America. He was a family man. And he was an outstanding racing driver. Somehow, he had this amazing ability to take it all in stride. He never seemed to be in a rush, except when he was in a racing car. In my career, he was the most outstanding all-around person I've ever met in racing. He was a really great person. He could manage to combine his family emotions with an outstanding business acumen and an ability to drive racing cars — all at the same time."

DEREK BELL

10-year-old Todd Holbert wears his father's victory medallion following the 1985 New York 500.

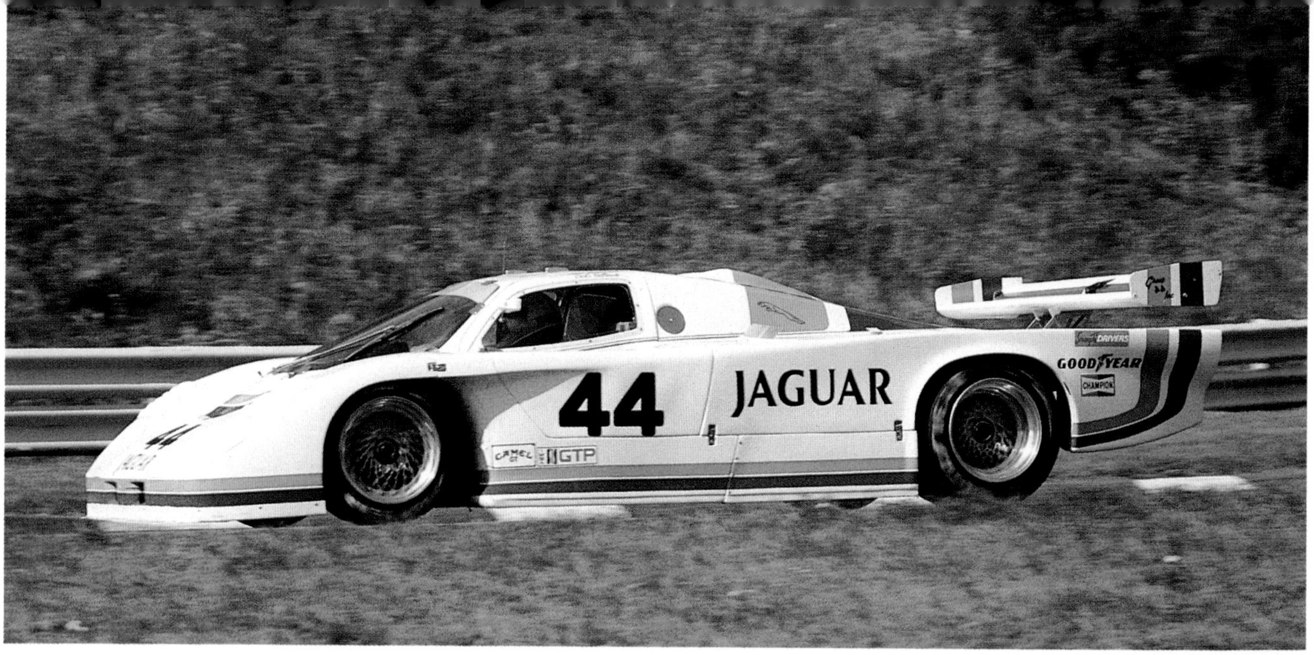

**(Top)** Long-time Glen competitor Bob Tullius fielded a pair of immaculately-prepared Jaguars for drivers including himself, Doc Bundy, Brian Redman, Hurley Haywood and Chip Robinson.

**(Above)** Drake Olson (left), in the Dyson Porsche 962, gets together with the Jiffy Lube Mazda of Steve Durst in turn two during the 1985 Camel Continental. Both cars were destroyed in the resulting 140 mph crash, with Durst suffering broken ribs. Ironically, both teams returned to win the respective Camel GTP and Camel Lights classes in the 1996 Camel Continental.

**(Right)** Aftermath of the violent Olson/Durst accident.

**(Top Left)** Pete Halsmer, Lyn St. James and Scott Pruett drove a pair of Budweiser Zakspeed Ford Mustang Probes in the 1986 New York 500.

**(Top Right)** One of the fastest of the early IMSA Camel GTP Prototypes was the Rick Hendrick-owned Corvette GTP, driven by South African Sarel van der Merwe.

**(Left)** Once a popular driver at The Glen, Dan Gurney returned as a very successful car owner in IMSA competition.

**(Lower Right)** Jack Baldwin (left) and NASCAR driver Geoff Bodine braved 100-degree heat to win the 1986 Camel Continental GTO class in a Chevy Camaro.

“My favorite Glen memory is definitely the year I raced with Geoff Bodine. We had a great race against Jack Roush and Scott Pruett and we got to stand on top of victory stand that day. It was an honor to drive with Geoff, he did a great job, and it was a hard fought battle — a tough race — and it was very satisfying to win that race. It was 100 degrees with 98 percent humidity. That was the one race I got covered with ice like a fish when I got out of the car. It was a tough race and a great effort.”

JACK BALDWIN

**(Top Left)** After competitive drives for Bob Tullius' Group 44 Jaguars and Al Holbert's Porsche, Chip Robinson moved to Nissan where he won the 1989 and 1990 Camel Continentals.

**(Top Right)** Faced with scheduling conflicts with Indy car and IROC races in Cleveland, Al Holbert and Derek Bell were joined by Jim Adams for the two-day Camel Continental in 1984. Adams adapted to the unfamiliar Porsche 962 to share the victory in The Glen's reopening race.

**(Center)** A pair of Nissan GTP ZXTs race into turn two in the 1990 Camel Continental VII. John Paul Jr. and Jacques Villeneuve (brother of the 1979 USGP winner) are in the BFGoodrich Nissan No. 67, with Geoff Brabham finishing fifth in the No. 1 car he shared with Derek Daly.

**(Below)** The Nissan GTP ZXT scored three consecutive Camel Continental GTP victories from 1988-90, driven by Geoff Brabham, Chip Robinson, John Morton and Bob Earl.

**(Above)** Four different marques battle in the 1991 Camel Continental VIII. Castrol Jaguar XJR-16 driver Davy Jones passes the pole-winning No. 7 Porsche 962C of Bernd Schneider and John Winter, followed by the Nissan 300ZXT of runner-up Geoff Brabham and eventual winner Juan Fangio in the No. 99 Toyota Eagle. In the background is the Jaguar XJR-16 of Raul Boesel.

**(Center Left)** John Andretti (second from left) and Davy Jones teamed to give BMW its first IMSA GTP victory in the 1986 Kodak Copier 500.

**(Left)** Davy Jones ran the fastest lap in North American road course history in qualifying for the 1992 Camel Continental. The native of nearby Cortland, N.Y. ran a lap of 58.699 seconds in Tom Walkinshaw's Bud Light Jaguar XJR-14 on the 2.45-mile circuit — newly configured with the Inner Loop. That's a speed of 150.334 mph!

It's one of my favorite racing tracks in the U.S. It's wonderful. Not only the racetrack itself, it's the fans, the atmosphere, it's a great weekend all together. I have very good memories from the past. It's one of those places that has all the tradition that you need.

JUAN MANUEL FANGIO II

**(Opposing Page)** Juan Fangio II of Argentina holds up the Steuben bowl trophy for winning the 1992 Camel Continental in Dan Gurney's All-American Racers Toyota Eagle Mk III. Fangio, the nephew of five-time World Champion Juan Fangio, won the race three straight times, from 1991-93.

**(Right)** Davy Jones won the pole for the 1992 Camel Continental IX with a lap of 150.334 mph, but Juan Fangio II won the race in Dan Gurney's Toyota Eagle Mk III.

**(Below Right)** P.J. Jones (left) won the pole for Camel Continental X in 1993, but Toyota Eagle Mk III teammate Juan Fangio won the finale for the Camel GT Prototypes at The Glen.

**(Top Left)** TV's "Coach," Craig T. Nelson meets a future fan at an autograph session. Nelson drove his own Lexus Spice World Sports Car at The Glen.

**(Top Right)** Jason Priestley of the TV show "Beverly Hills 90210" did double duty at The Glen, driving Ford Mustangs in both the Endurance Championship and GT series.

**(Above Right)** Tom Cruise drove in The Glen SCCA Finger Lakes National in 1987, retiring Bob Sharp's Nissan after an early accident.

**(Left)** Walter Payton, the leading rusher in NFL history, takes time to sign autographs before competing in the 1992 Trans-Am. His best moment at The Glen was in the 1989 SCCA Pro Sports 2000 race, when he spun on the first turn of the first lap and shattered the track record on a strong drive back through the field.

**(Above)** Five-time IMSA champion Irv Hoerr of Peoria, Ill., scored a pair of triumphs in the IMSA Kelly American Challenge Series. The Oldsmobile driver returned to score three straight GT victories in IMSA competition at The Glen from 1994-96.

**(Top Right)** The IMSA Firestone Firehawk Endurance Championship series held eight 24-hour races at The Glen, from 1985 through 1992. Above is a typical scene from all-night racing.

**(Center Left)** The little car that could — John Andretti, Ron Christensen and car owner Ray Korman drove this BMW 325e to an overall victory in the 1986 Seagrams Coolers 24 Hours, the biggest upset in Firestone Firehawk history.

**(Center Right)** Tom Kendall captured overall honors (with Max Jones) in the 1986 Firestone Firehawk 500 in a Nissan 300ZXT, and came back the following day to place second in the GTU division of the Kodak Copier 500. The future star captured championships in both IMSA divisions that year.

**(Right)** The winning Camaro of Joe Varde, Doug Goad and Bob Kahn is greeted by a bridge filled with waving checkered flags.

"It's a great race course. It came upon hard times, and now it's back on the surge again, that's great. It's one of the half-dozen great race courses in the country. It certainly gets your attention.

"There are always a good bunch of people up there, and the track has such an incredible history. I'm just delighted to be part of it in some small way."

PAUL NEWMAN

**(Top)** Wally Dallenbach drives this Jack Roush Mercury Capri to victory in the 1985 Chase Lincoln First Trans-Am.

**(Center Left)** Willy T. Ribbs won the SCCA Trans-Am in 1984. He would return to The Glen in 1988 to win the IMSA Kodak Copier 500, driving Dan Gurney's All-American Racers Toyota Celica.

**(Center Right)** Wally Dallenbach Jr. followed up a fourth place finish in the 1984 Glen Trans-Am by winning the 1985 event.

**(Right)** Bob Sharp Racing teammates Jim Fitzgerald (left) and Paul Newman share a light moment with Willy T. Ribbs prior to the 1985 Trans-Am. Newman won the pole and finished second in that event, and also won an SCCA National race from the pole the same day.

**(Top Left)** Al Unser Jr. dominated the five visits of the International Race of Champions to Watkins Glen International. He won in 1986, 1988, and 1989, finished second in 1987, and third in 1991. Unser celebrates winning both the race and IROC title in 1986.

**(Top Right)** Mario Andretti (left) returned to The Glen for the 1987 IROC finale, joined by his son Michael — a top Indy car driver. Mario finished sixth, two positions ahead of Michael.

**(Above Right)** The podium finishers from the 1987 IROC finale. Left to right are runner-up Al Unser Jr., winner and champion Geoff Bodine and third place finisher Bobby Rahal.

**(Center Left)** Geoff Bodine, in the tan Camaro, takes the lead from Al Unser Jr. (in the pink car) en route to winning The Glen's 1987 IROC finale and series championship.

**(Left)** Wally Dallenbach leads a group of cars in 1987 IROC action.

**(Top)** Tommy Kendall kept his Trans-Am winning streak alive with a victory in the 1997 Serengeti Eyewear Trans-Am. That tied him with Mark Donohue, whose streak ended at The Glen when Jerry Titus won in 1968. Ironically, Kendall ended the year by winning the Jerry Titus Award, voted by the American Auto Racing Writers and Broadcasters Association.

**(Above)** Car owner Jack Roush quietly observes the Victory Circle festivities following Kendall's victory.

**(Left)** Sporting bleached blonde hair, Tommy Kendall climbs from his car after winning the 1997 Serengeti Eyewear Trans-Am.

Winning the 1997 Trans-Am race was my biggest moment at The Glen. It was obviously sweet because of all that has happened to me at The Glen, my injuries and so forth, along with breaking Mark Donohue's record for consecutive Trans-Am victories. It was kind of fitting to set the record at The Glen, because to break Mark Donohue's record I had to win at the track he was unable to win at (in 1969).

TOMMY KENDALL

**(Top Left)** Dodge driver Tommy Archer (No. 3) leads the Camaros of Scott Sharp (No. 33) and eventual winner Jack Baldwin (No. 25) during the 1992 Snap-On Tools Trans-Am.

**(Top Right)** Scott Sharp leads the field in the Rain-X Camaro en route to winning the 1993 Trans-Am during the Bud at the Glen weekend.

**(Center)** Jack Baldwin (center) celebrates his last-lap victory in Buz McCall's Hot Wheels Camaro in the 1992 Snap-on Tools Trans-Am. Scott Sharp (right) led the first 41 circuits in McCall's Duracell Camaro, only to tangle with a lapped car in turn 10 — which cost him not only the victory but the season championship. Taking third in a Whistler Ford Mustang is Jim Stevens.

**(Lower Left)** Dorsey Schroeder was a winner in the IMSA Firestone Firehawk and Camel GTO divisions before winning the 1995 Glen Trans-Am. The popular driver also is a regular Winston Cup competitor at The Glen.

**(Lower Right)** Canadian Ron Fellows won the Trans-Am races in 1994 and 1995, but his biggest Glen victory came in the 1997 Parts America 150, when he won in his first ever start in NASCAR's Craftsman Truck Series.

It's a special event every time we go to The Glen. I always find myself at midnight or 1 a.m. driving around the old circuit real fast. It's a special circuit, and I always enjoy going there.

BRIAN CUNNINGHAM

**(Above)** Eliseo Salazar and Gianpiero Moretti combined to win the final race of the original three hour Continental format in 1994 in the Momo Ferrari 333SP. Above, Salazar leads Jeremy Dale in the Motorola Olds Spice in early action.

**(Top Left)** Javier Quiros, Boris Said and Pete Halsmer finished second in GTS-2 in the 1996 First Union Six Hours in Tom Milner's First Union/Valvoline BMW M3.

**(Center Left)** After a pair of solo GTS-1 victories in the three-hour Glen Continentals of 1994 and 1995, Irv Hoerr took his third straight victory in the 1996 First Union Six Hours. Co-driving the Brix Racing Olds Aurora were Darin Brassfield, Brian Cunningham and Brian Devries. Cunningham, who set the fastest lap in his class, is the grandson of Glen pioneer Briggs Cunningham and son of Briggs Cunningham III, who also competed in the streets of The Glen.

**(Left)** The GTS-1 winning Ford Panoz GTR-1 of Andy Wallace, David Brabham and Doc Bundy during the 1997 First Union Six Hours. Brabham, the son of Sir Jack Brabham, made a successful Glen debut, joining his brother Geoff as a winner at WGI.

**(Above)** Watkins Glen returned to a familiar format with the running of the 1996 First Union Six Hours. Max Papis jumps to the lead in the Momo Ferrari 333SP, and he would still be in front at the finish, six hours later.

**(Left)** Max Papis, in the Momo Ferrari 333SP, leads the Dyson Ford of Andy Wallace during the 1996 First Union Six Hours.

**(Lower Left)** Max Papis wears the funny hat while car owner/co-driver Gianpiero Moretti waves the Italian flag following their popular victory in the 1996 First Union Six Hours.

**(Opposing Page Middle)** Sports car races go on rain or shine. Rob Dyson's Riley and Scott Ford Mk III leads the action up through the Esses during their victorious drive in the 1997 First Union Six Hours.

**(Opposing Page Lower)** Butch Leitzinger, James Weaver and Rob Dyson celebrate victory in the 1997 First Union Six Hours, sanctioned by Professional SportsCar Racing.

rain-X
EXXON
BOSCH
20
DYSON
Hella
PAGID
GOODYEAR
rain-X
16

Zippo
FIRST UNION
EXXON
BOSCH
DYSON
Hella
SVO
20
GOODYEAR

FIRST UNION
SIX HOURS
of The Glen
GOODYEAR
OMP
ROLEX 24
BOSCH Spark Plugs

**(Top Left)**The 1989 U.S. Vintage Grand Prix featured the largest gathering of Ford GT40s up to that time.

**(Top Right)** On-track action during the 1990 Can-Am Reunion.

**(Center Left)** Racing returns to the streets! The 1949 Grand Prix-winning Ardent Alligator, now owned by Peter McManus, leads a Cunningham C4R "continuation model" during the 1997 Grand Prix Festival in the village of Watkins Glen during the Zippo U.S. Vintage Grand Prix.

**(Center Middle)** A large field of Trans-Am cars are lined up in the pits to highlight the 1995 Zippo U.S. Vintage Grand Prix.

**(Center Right)** Past and present leaders at the Glen. Mal Currie (left), former Executive Director of the Grand Prix Corporation, and Watkins Glen International President John Saunders participate in the dedication of the original Start/Finish Line marker in front of the Schuyler County Court House in 1989.

**(Right)** A key component of the annual Grand Prix Festival is the Race Reenactment on the original 6.6-mile downtown circuit.

# NASCAR Comes North

## The Road Warriors of NASCAR

NASCAR stock car racing wasn't new to Watkins Glen. In fact, the first professional race ever held at the circuit was a Grand National race in 1957, with NASCAR's top echelon returning to The Glen in 1964 and 1965. NASCAR-type late modifieds and late models competed at The Glen in 1975. But stock car racing — along with motorcycles, snowmobiles and go-karts — was nearly totally eclipsed by the major sports car and formula car racing at the circuit.

When Watkins Glen International announced the return of NASCAR with the 1986 Bud at The Glen Winston Cup race, many wondered how stock car fans would accept the notion of running the primarily oval track series on a road circuit. They had their answer one week prior to the inaugural Bud at The Glen, when fans began lining up on the roads of Schuyler County to anticipate the opening of the gates.

A crowd estimated at over 88,000 witnessed Tim Richmond win the first Bud at The Glen, and that was just the beginning. Crowds swelled as the Bud at The Glen was established as New York State's largest motorsports event, witnessing fantastic racing on the famed road course.

"I was very happy to see NASCAR go back there," said Ned Jarrett, who competed at The Glen in 1964 and 1965. "I felt it was needed for the growth of NASCAR Winston Cup racing to be in that market, and at a track that had so much tradition, so it was exciting to go back and work the races and see the Winston Cup cars."

A large crowd watches as the field of Winston Cup competitors prepares to take the green flag for the 1986 Bud at The Glen, and a new era in Watkins Glen racing history begins.

**(Above)** Prior to 1986, Watkins Glen held three races for NASCAR's Grand National (now Winston Cup) division. Buck Baker won in 1957, the first professional race in Glen history. Above, pole-sitter Billy Wade (No. 1 Mercury) leads the Ford of Ned Jarrett into the first turn after taking the green flag for the 1964 race.

**(Right)** Billy Wade (left) and car owner Bud Moore after the 1964 NASCAR Grand National race, won by Wade in a Mercury. It was his fourth consecutive Grand National victory. Wade lost his life six months later during a tire test at Daytona.

"It's nice to see it's progressed to that point where NASCAR is now the popular racing at The Glen," added Jarrett, now a popular television commentator. "It isn't surprising to see that progression, because of the interest in Winston Cup racing, but it's very gratifying, especially with the great names, American and international, that have raced at Watkins Glen over the years. To have the sport that I've been involved with all my life to go to Watkins Glen and become number one at that very historic track is very, very meaningful."

Ricky Rudd survived a fender-banging last lap challenge from Rusty Wallace to win in 1988, with his victory sandwiched between a pair of Wallace triumphs at The Glen. Ernie Irvan saw rivals Davey Allison and Mark Martin spin in the first turn on the final lap en route to winning in 1991. Mark Martin began his three-year winning streak when Kyle Petty and Dale Earnhardt tangled in the Esses late in the 1993 event, with Martin running down upset-minded Wally Dallenbach late in the 1995 race.

**(Above)** Ned Jarrett (No. 11) chases eventual 1964 winner Billy Wade as the pair lap the Chevy of Roy Tyner (No. 9) entering the final turn — which is near the site of today's first turn. Bernie Alvarez is driving the No. 10 Ford. Jarrett ran near the front until a blown engine sidelined him in the closing laps, although he still finished eighth.

**(Right)** The field heads up the Esses after the start of the 1965 Grand National event, The Glen's final NASCAR race until the inaugural Bud at The Glen in 1986.

**(Below)** Marvin Panch wears the laurel wreath after winning the 1965 NASCAR Grand National race for the Wood Brothers.

Geoff Bodine, a native of nearby Chemung who once climbed a tree overlooking the backstraight to watch the U.S. Grand Prix, took an emotional victory in 1996, in a performance overshadowed by Dale Earnhardt. Recovering from serious injuries suffered less than two weeks earlier, Earnhardt won the pole at track record speed and went on to lead the most laps, finishing sixth.

The success of the Bud at The Glen prompted the addition of other NASCAR divisions, including the Busch Grand National, Craftsman Trucks, Featherlite Modifieds and Busch North. All of them have enjoyed crowd support and very competitive racing.

Jeff Gordon, NASCAR's newest superstar capped the 50th year of racing at the circuit by winning the 1997 Bud at The Glen.

In closing this retrospective on The Glen's first half-century of competition, it's only fitting to turn to the man whose dream was realized with the running of the 1948 Grand Prix.

"The NASCAR stock cars are the greatest cars racing in our country today," said Cameron Argetsinger, who practices law in downtown Montour Falls, only a stone's throw from the race circuit. "Always, in 1948 and in every year since then, the best cars running have raced at Watkins Glen."

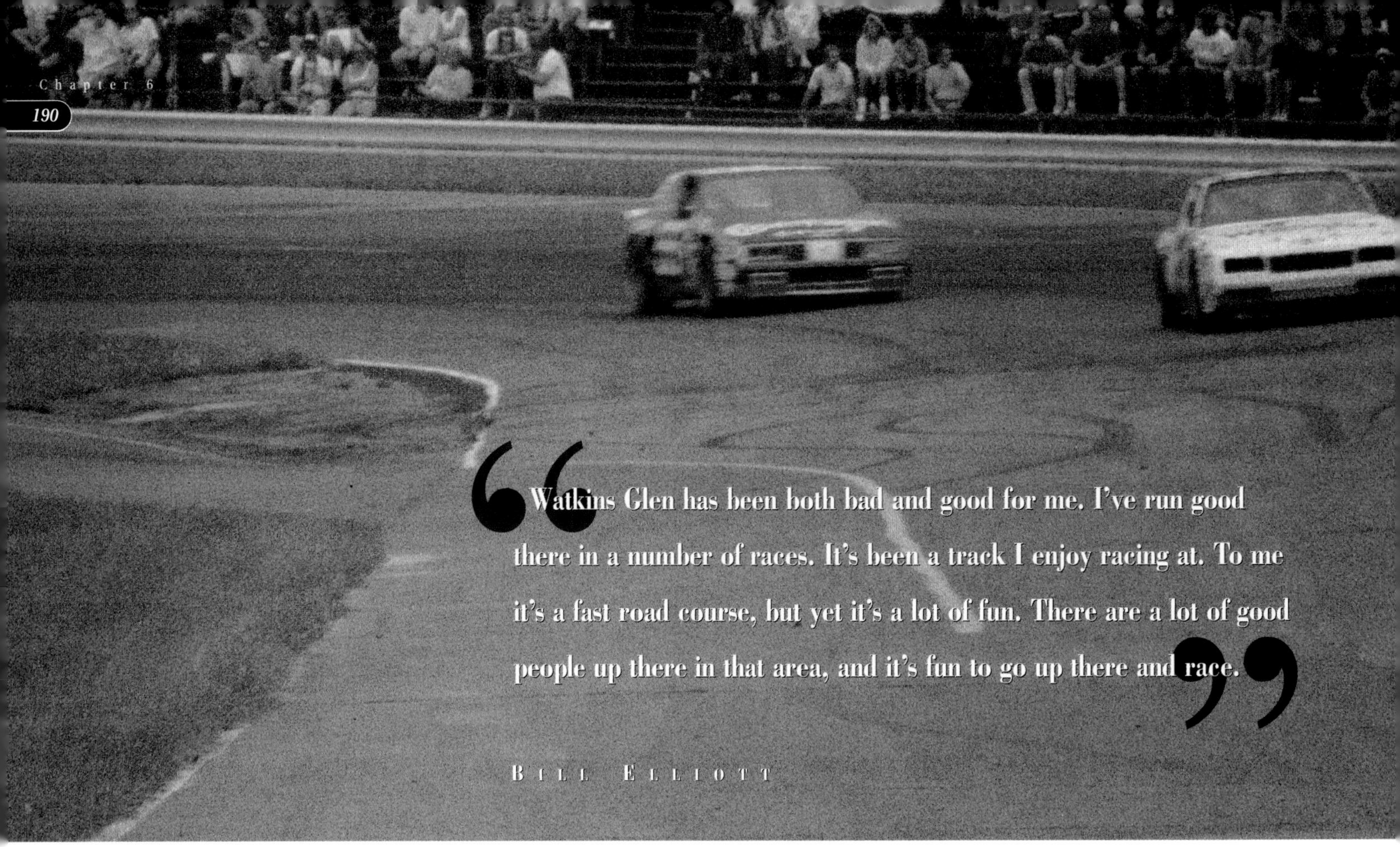

"Watkins Glen has been both bad and good for me. I've run good there in a number of races. It's been a track I enjoy racing at. To me it's a fast road course, but yet it's a lot of fun. There are a lot of good people up there in that area, and it's fun to go up there and race."

BILL ELLIOTT

**(Above)** Geoff Bodine holds off Tim Richmond and Darrell Waltrip in the inaugural Bud at The Glen. Bodine challenged for the victory until an engine problem caused him to spin in turn one late in the race. He would have to wait 10 years until he finally scored a hometown Winston Cup victory.

**(Center)** A large crowd watches the field race up the Esses in the 1986 Bud at The Glen.

**(Below)** NASCAR founder William H.G. France (center) and his son, William C. France, meet with Dale Earnhardt prior to the 1987 IROC finale. The Frances' International Speedway Corporation teamed with Corning Enterprises to revive racing at Watkins Glen.

**(Left)** While Bill Elliott was fastest down the back straight in qualifying for the 1986 Bud at The Glen, he failed to negotiate turn five. Elliott supervises the loading of his wrecked Coors Thunderbird onto a flatbed.

**(Below)** Bill Elliott managed to qualify 22nd in his repaired race car, and went on to finish fourth in the inaugural Bud at The Glen, losing third to a daring pass by Dale Earnhardt in the closing laps.

**(Left)** Tim Richmond leads Rusty Wallace in the first Bud at The Glen. Richmond went on to win in the Hendrick Racing Folgers Chevy, while Wallace finished a strong sixth in the Alugard Pontiac.

**(Below)** A jubilant Tim Richmond gets a Budweiser shower from his crew following his 1986 victory.

**(Opposing Page)** Tim Richmond seemed to be headed for superstardom following his 1986 victory. He made only one more Glen appearance, finishing 10th in 1987, and died in seclusion on the day of the 1989 Bud at The Glen.

Looking back at that (1988) finish with Ricky Rudd, I'll never forget that. He got alongside of me in the last turn heading to the Start/Finish line. I finally gave him a good bump in the rear end, tried to get him sideways, and got underneath him. He saw me and blocked me off. I think my whole car was off in the grass heading to the Start/Finish line. It looked pretty exciting. The Glen's been good to me, and The Glen's been bad to me, but every time I go there I'm always excited and I have a great time.

RUSTY WALLACE

(Top) Four Winston Cup champions race into turn one. Dale Earnhardt leads Bill Elliott, Darrell Waltrip and Rusty Wallace.

(Above) Rusty Wallace returned to Victory Circle in the 1989 Bud at The Glen, finishing one second ahead of Mark Martin.

(Right) Rusty Wallace holds the first place trophy after winning the 1987 Bud at The Glen. Wallace was King of the Road at Watkins Glen in the late Eighties.

Motorcraft
THUNDERBIRD
KODIAK
27
PONTIAC

ston Cup Series

**(Top Spread)** Geoff Bodine holds the lead in the 1988 Bud at The Glen, followed by Rusty Wallace, Ricky Rudd, Bill Elliott and Terry Labonte.

**(Opposing Page)** Rusty Wallace tried to squeeze his way to Victory Circle in 1988, but Ricky Rudd in the Quaker State Buick was not to be denied in the most exciting finish of the Bud at The Glen. If the two crashed — which nearly happened — Bill Elliott was right there in third place.

**(Right)** Ricky and Linda Rudd share the spotlight in Victory Circle following the 1988 Bud at The Glen.

**(Top)** Ernie Irvan and Mark Martin battle to the white flag during the 1991 Bud at The Glen. The race was decided in turn one, when Martin's Folgers Ford and Davy Allison's Havoline Ford both spun. Ricky Rudd finished second in the Tide Chevy, followed by Martin. Ted Musgrave made his Watkins Glen debut in the No. 55 Tops Markets Pontiac, finishing 26th.

**(Above)** Ernie Irvan's Kodak Chevy is already in front of the Red, White and Blue Grandstands as Mark Martin (Folgers Ford) and Davey Allison spin in turn one during the 1991 Bud at The Glen.

**(Left)** Ernie Irvan won the 1991 Bud at The Glen in the Kodak Chevy, and returned to The Glen the following spring to win the Fay's 150 Busch Grand National race.

**(Left)** Kyle Petty leads Dale Earnhardt up the Esses during the 1992 Bud at The Glen. Petty won the rain-shortened race over Morgan Shepherd and Mark Martin. A year later, Petty and Earnhardt crashed in the Esses while fighting for the lead, handing the victory to Martin.

**(Below)** Kyle Petty takes home the trophy for the 1992 Bud at The Glen in the Mello Yello Pontiac, called after 51 laps due to rain.

(**Above**) Mark Martin prior to scoring a second place finish in the 1989 Bud at The Glen, his first top-10 finish at the circuit. It was his first of nine consecutive top-five finishes at The Glen through 1997.

(**Above Right**) Mark Martin's primary car was destroyed in a violent wreck with Dick Trickle and Troy Beebe in Thursday practice prior to the 1990 Bud at The Glen. He went to a backup and finished fifth in the Folgers Ford.

(**Right**) Mark Martin leads the field down the front straight following the green flag for the 1993 Bud at The Glen — Martin's first of three consecutive Glen triumphs from the Busch Pole.

**(Top)** Mark Martin leads into turn two.

**(Right)** Mark Martin joined the legends of The Glen by scoring three consecutive victories in the Bud at The Glen.

"The first year we sat on the pole in '93, I had no idea we could run that fast. I thought they had made a mistake when they gave me my time after qualifying. But it's an awesome feeling. Each year was like a snowball. Each year when we sat on the pole and won the race, it was like a dream come true. We want to start that all over again."

MARK MARTIN

**(Above)** A few of Mark Martin's fans celebrate his "3-Peat."

**(Left)** Wally Dallenbach Jr. won the 1985 Glen Trans-Am, and came back to score a pair of second place finishes behind Mark Martin in the 1993 and 1995 Bud at The Glen.

**(Below)** Wally Dallenbach had a one-off ride in Bill Davis' MBNA Pontiac for the 1995 Bud at The Glen, and he nearly drove it to Victory Circle. A late caution for Todd Bodine's blown engine allowed Mark Martin to catch up and eventually win.

**(Opposing Page)** Habit forming? Mark Martin takes the trophy for the third straight year in 1995.

NASCAR
Winston C
Budweiser
Budweiser
Budweiser
Budweiser
Kendall GT
MOTOR OIL
PEPSI
Valvoline
Cummins
Valvoline
Cummins
Gatorade
NASCAR
RACE CAR
NASCAR
Winston Cup
BUSCH
Gatorade
PYROIL
PYROIL
© VALVOLINE, INC. 1991
ZEREX
MAC TOOLS
apac
BOSCH
QUARTER MASTER
SPEED-PRO
sikkens
COMPETITION CAMS
JESEL

**(Top Left)** Richard Petty — NASCAR's "King" first raced at The Glen in 1964, and returned to complete all but two possible laps in the first seven runnings of the Bud at The Glen.

**(Top Right)** 1973 Winston Cup champion Benny Parsons made several appearances in the Bud at The Glen before launching a successful career as a television commentator.

**(Above)** IndyCar legend A.J. Foyt made only one visit to The Glen in 1989, but drove in two races. He finished 10th in Saturday's IROC race, and returned to run Sunday's Bud at The Glen. He had a short day, blowing the engine in his Copenhagen Oldsmobile after only seven laps.

**(Left)** Darrell Waltrip finished 18th in the 1997 Bud at The Glen. One of the most consistent drivers in Glen NASCAR history, Waltrip completed all 861 possible laps in 10 Watkins Glen starts. His best finish was a second in the 1986 Bud at The Glen.

**(Above)** Davey Allison was just starting to come into his own as a road racer before his untimely death in a 1993 helicopter accident. He finished 10th in the 1991 Bud at The Glen.

**(Right)** While Bill Elliott has yet to win the Bud at The Glen, the popular Georgian captured the 1993 Fay's 150 Busch Grand National race.

**(Below)** Dale Jarrett qualified second for the 1997 Bud at The Glen, and led the first 14 laps, but transmission trouble led to a 32nd place finish, which ultimately cost him the Winston Cup championship to Jeff Gordon.

**(Below Right)** Brothers Bobby (left) and Terry Labonte relax prior to the 1995 Bud at The Glen.

**(Left)** Curtis Markham heads up the Esses in the Lysol Pontiac heading towards an eighth place finish during the 1995 Lysol 200 NASCAR Busch Series race. That was the first year Lysol sponsored the event, which was lengthened to 200 miles, and the beginning of a successful partnership.

**(Below)** Terry Labonte on his way to the first of three consecutive Lysol 200 victories. Labonte dominated the event, leading 41 of the 62 laps. Kenny Wallace, who led six laps before blowing an engine on lap 57, follows Labonte into turn one.

**(Top Left)** Intense bumper-to-bumper racing down the front straight in Busch Series action at The Glen.

**(Top Right)** Young guns — Jeff Gordon (left) and Todd Bodine chat prior to the 1991 Fay's 150. Bodine finished fifth in the Fay's Drug Stores Buick, one position ahead of Gordon's Carolina Ford Dealers Ford.

**(Above)** Bill Elliott celebrates his victory in the 1993 Fay's 150. Elliott won over Terry Labonte, Ward Burton, Joe Nemechek and Todd Bodine in his Budweiser Ford.

**(Left)** Chad Little, driving the Bayer Ford, gave Terry Labonte and the No. 14 MW Windows Chevy all he could handle in 1995. Little led twice for 42 laps, but had to settle for second place, 3.88 seconds behind Labonte.

**(Left)** Mike Dillion's crew changes tires and refuels his car in a 20 second ballet — NASCAR style. The coordinated teamwork of a pit stop is always exciting to watch.

**(Center)** David Green leads Hermie Sadler, Michael Waltrip, Kenny Wallace, eventual winner Terry Labonte and Todd Bodine out of turn 11 onto the frontstretch during the 1996 Lysol 200. An exciting race saw Green swap the lead with Labonte, Waltrip and Bodine before finishing 5th, on his way to the 1996 Busch Series Championship.

**(Below)** Terry Labonte sprays The Glenora Champagne after winning his third consecutive Lysol 200 in 1996.

(Top) Mike McLaughlin leads Jason Keller up the Esses during the 1997 Lysol 200.

(Left) Friendly rivals and teammates Mike McLaughlin (right) and Todd Bodine wave to each other heading up the Esses on the cool-down lap of the 1997 Lysol 200.

(Lower Left) Mike McLaughlin leaps from his Royal Oak Chevy and into the arms of his crew in Victory Circle.

(Below) The local team won the 1997 Lysol 200. The Team 34 Chevy, owned by Elmira businessmen and driven by Mike McLaughlin of Waterloo, N.Y., edged out teammate Todd Bodine of Chemung, N.Y. Left to right are Jeff Welliver, McLaughlin, Scott Welliver and Frank Cicci in Victory Circle.

(Top) The debut of the NASCAR Busch North Series in 1993 was one of the most competitive races in Glen history. Mike McLaughlin spun while leading a tight pack in the closing laps, leading to a fantastic three-wide finish out of the final turn. Above, Curtis Markham in the Skoal Pontiac leads eventual winner Bobby Dragon in the Fisher Snow Plows 125.

(Above) Canadian Victor Sifton escaped serious injury in this wild finish to the 1995 Burnham Boilers 150. Winner Joe Bessey has already taken the checkered flag, while Curtis Markham (No. 63 Lysol Pontiac) takes fourth.

(Right) Eventual winner Ted Christopher (No. 13) takes the green flag for the 1997 Burnham Boilers 150. Canadian Kat Teasdale (No. 94) ran second in the early going before mechanical problems kept her from a strong finish.

**(Above)** Andy Santerre scores a popular victory in the 1996 Burnham Boilers 150.

**(Above Right)** Mike Stefanik carries the sponsor's colors in the Burnham Boilers 150. The Rhode Island driver won both the NASCAR Busch North and Featherlite Modified Series Championship titles in 1997.

**(Right)** Ted Christopher celebrates his 1997 Busch North victory after emerging from the LesCare Kitchens Chevrolet.

**(Top Center)** NASCAR Featherlite Modifieds tackle the Inner Loop.

**(Mid Center)** Championship-bound Mike Stefanik leads the field into turn one, heading for his second consecutive late summer modified victory at The Glen.

**(Lower Center)** Mike Stefanik takes the checkered flag in a narrow victory over Rick Fuller in the 1997 Ruffles 150.

**(Below)** NASCAR-style modifieds first raced at the Glen in 1975 as part of the Kendall 250 doubleheader with late model stock cars.

**(Bottom)** Former Ithaca College quarterback Tim Connolly of Endicott, N.Y., scored a popular home track triumph in the 1997 Polaroid 125 in the Tidy Cat/Garbarino Dodge.

**(Top)** Two poles in one day! Steve Park caught everyone's attention by capturing the Busch Pole for the 1996 NASCAR Craftsman Truck Series Parts America 150 in a "pinch hit" role for Joe Nemechek, and came back an hour later to win the pole for the Featherlite Modified race. Left to right are Big Joe Nemechek, Martha Nemechek, Nemco Motorsports crew chief George Church, and Park.

**(Above)** Mike Stefanik and his crew pose in Victory Circle following their victory in the 1997 Ruffles 150.

**(Top)** Boris Said, a second-generation road racer at The Glen, leads a pack of NASCAR Craftsman Trucks through the first turn during the 1997 Parts America 150.

**(Center)** Mike Skinner struggles to keep up as eventual winner Ron Hornaday leads Geoff Bodine in the inaugural Parts America 150 in 1996.

**(Left)** A NAPA crewman manages to do what the competition failed to do in 1996 — cool off eventual Series champion Ron Hornaday following his Parts America 150 victory. Hornaday took the points lead with the victory, and never gave it up.

**(Top)** Two Trans-Am vets pace the field in the 1997 Parts America 150 — Canadian Ron Fellows and Dorsey Schroeder.

**(Far Left)** A jubilant Ron Fellows celebrates his upset victory in the 1997 Parts America 150, his NASCAR debut.

**(Left)** Linda Fellows congratulates her husband following his Parts America 150 triumph.

**(Right)** "It hurts so good," Dale Earnhardt told the press following his Busch Pole-winning run.

**(Below)** Despite suffering a broken collarbone and sternum in a horrifying flip at Talladega two weeks earlier, Dale Earnhardt won the pole for the 1996 Bud at The Glen. He had David Green ready to relief drive at his first pit stop.

**(Bottom)** Deciding he felt good enough to race, Dale Earnhardt led the most laps in the 1996 Bud at The Glen, although he faded late in the race to finish sixth in a solo drive.

**(Opposing Page)** Dale Earnhardt — NASCAR's "Intimidator" is a three-time pole winner for the Bud at The Glen.

# "It hurts so good!"

DALE EARNHARDT

Busch Pole winner for the 1996 Bud at The Glen, two weeks after suffering serious injuries in an accident at Talladega.

**(Top Left)** Dale Jarrett leads Jeff Gordon and Kyle Petty during the 1996 Bud at The Glen.

**(Top Right)** Ken Schrader leads the 1996 Bud at The Glen in Rick Hendrick's Budweiser Chevy — but second place Geoff Bodine is not to be denied his home track victory.

**(Left)** Geoff Bodine leads the 1996 Bud at The Glen in his QVC Ford Thunderbird.

**(Bottom Left)** A jubilant Geoff Bodine celebrates.

**(Opposing Page)** He once watched the races from atop a tree near the backstraight. He raced snowmobiles and modifieds, and won in IMSA sports cars and IROC. In 1996, Geoff Bodine won the biggest race at his home track, the Bud at The Glen. Bodine holds the Riesbeck Cup in Victory Circle, the Steuben Bowl named after his good friend Jim Riesbeck, the Corning Inc. executive who brought racing back to The Glen in 1984 and passed away in 1993.

"Nothing compares to winning a NASCAR Winston Cup race, especially winning at home. It was the fulfillment of a long time goal and it was a relief to finally win the Bud at The Glen. That victory ended two bad years for me personally and professionally, and it opened up a new chapter in my life. It was like a fresh start.

**(Top)** Todd Bodine was a surprise winner of the Busch Pole Award for the 1997 Bud at The Glen, giving his Busch Series car owners — Frank Cicci and Scott and Jeff Welliver — the pole in their first Winston Cup start.

**(Above)** Geoff Bodine came close to a repeat victory in the 1997 Bud at The Glen, but finished second behind Jeff Gordon. Above, he leads Jeff Gordon and Rusty Wallace, who finished third, up the Esses in the QVC Ford. The three drivers swapped the lead all day.

**(Top Center Spread)** Todd Bodine, driving the Hardinge Chevrolet, and Dale Jarrett lead the field into turn eleven prior to the start of the 1997 Bud at The Glen.

**(Mid-Center Spread)** Fans in the new Pit Terrace watch the intense pit stop action during the 1997 Bud at The Glen.

**(Lower Center Spread)** There's good racing through the pack down the front straight heading into turn one during the 1997 Bud at The Glen.

**(Top)** Jeff Gordon takes the checkered flag, winning the 1997 Bud at The Glen.

"Watkins Glen is a great course. It really suits Winston Cup cars. You can get really aggressive here, but it's a mental thing. You have a problem here and all of a sudden you get a wake up call. The Bud at The Glen was one of the most satisfying wins I've ever had."

JEFF GORDON

Jeff Gordon scored his first career road course victory in the 1997 Bud at The Glen.

*In its rise from ragged infancy in 1948, to its position as America's premier road racing facility, Watkins Glen surely qualifies as one of the most outstanding and unlikely success stories in all of sports. The story that is Watkins Glen International continues to be written fifty years later.*